DISCOVERING GOD'S WILL IN YOUR LIFE

LLOYD JOHN OGILVIE

HARVEST HOUSE PUBLISHERS
Eugene, Oregon 97402

DISCOVERING GOD'S WILL IN YOUR LIFE.

Copyright © 1982 by Harvest House Publishers
Eugene, Oregon 97402
Formerly *God's Will in Your Life*

Library of Congress Catalog Card Number 82-082161
ISBN 0-89081-282-9

Printed in the United States of America.

CONTENTS

PREFACE

"I don't want to write a preface," wrote G. Campbell Morgan in his book on the Acts of the Apostles. He wanted to plunge right into his exposition of Acts! I can appreciate his feelings as I approach the subject of God's will for our lives.

But, unlike Morgan, I do want to write this preface. My main desire is to communicate my excitement about knowing and doing the will of God. There is no more important subject when seen in the light of God's purpose, power, and plan for each of us. We all want to be sure we are in the will of God and to receive guidance for our daily choices and decisions. We remember unguided decisions and the pain they caused us and the people around us. We also can reflect on those times when we felt caught up in the fast-moving currents of God's will and knew we were being guided. We were blessed, and so were the people and situations of our lives.

The essential discovery I want to share throughout this book is that the desire to know God's will is the result of His much greater desire to reveal it to us. He is in search of us. He creates the longing to want our lives to be maximum. As Henry Drummond has said, "The maximum achievement of any man's life after it is all over is to have done the will of God. No man or woman can have done any more with a life."

But that means more than guidance for each day. As we shall see, God's will is that we know

Him, live in an intimate relationship with Him, and as a result love, glorify, serve, and obey Him. My hope is that this discussion will clarify that more vividly and will also provide practical steps in knowing God's personal will for you.

Now a word about style. Throughout these chapters you will see such phrases as "At this point you're probably saying" or "Your question now is likely to be" or "Allow me to be very personal in sharing my experience of that truth." These expressions are part of what I hope will be a conversation between you and me as you read what I have written. My many talks with people about the will of God over the years have been on my mind all through the writing. I've heard you say, "Now wait a minute" or "If that's true, what about this?" or "That's exciting; press on!"

I have studied the Scriptures on the will of God, read dozens of history's great thinkers on the subject, and gathered illustrations from the lives of real people in preparation for a conversation with you about this supremely important subject. As I prepared, I had the questions sounding in my soul that people have asked me about knowing the will of God in their lives. My selection of material and theme development was in response to these.

Sometime during that preparation the idea hit me: Why not write the book as a one-to-one conversation? It would be something like a talk I might have with a close friend who asked, "Lloyd, tell me—how can I find God's will for my life?"

The task of writing became an exciting one! Instead of merely composing a book, it felt like an on-the-edge-of-our-chairs, eye-to-eye, mind-to-mind, heart-to-heart exchange. The questions I heard you asking were those I've heard asked repeatedly. Then new ones surfaced from within myself as I grappled with the implications of truths for our lives.

The result was that my pen would not move fast enough as my mind raced on and my eyes darted back and forth from the Bible to my writing pad. My concern was not rhetoric or carefully balanced sentences as much as it was the desire to communicate what the Lord was saying. What I felt compelled to do was faithfully listen to what God was saying in the Bible, share the fresh insights His Spirit gave, and empathize with the concerns I think you're experiencing about God's will and guidance.

As I wrote I felt I had been given the privilege of talking about the most important subject in the world with a real person who had great potential and authentic hopes. My prayer is that this purpose in writing will be accomplished to help you in a personal and practical way in your adventure of living God's will.

I want to express my gratitude to two people for their help in my preparation. My thanks to Kathy Guzman and Jack McNary, who helped me gather up materials for study prior to my writing. Special appreciation is given for Mrs. Guzman's faithful typing and preparation of the manuscript for publication.

Now let's press on together in the assurance that any time we want to know and do God's will, it is because He has called us into the quest.

—Lloyd John Ogilvie

1

The Wonder of the Will

My eagerness to write this book about the will of God, and your interest in reading it, says something about both of us. Also, it tells us something very significant about God and what He is up to in our lives. The longing to know God's will is a gift. His Spirit has been at work in us creating the desire to discover His will. He is the Initiator of our quest. That's the premise with which we begin. It will be woven all through everything I want to say.

I suspect that your interest is in finding daily guidance. We will be talking a lot about that. But one of the great discoveries of my life is that guidance is possible only after a deeper understanding and response to the ultimate will of God. We will get into specifics about guidance as they flow out of that. The last two chapters are devoted to the need for clarity for our ongoing choices and decisions. And I think we will be prepared to seek guidance in a much more creative and successful way. Now let's launch out into the deep, where the sailing gets exciting. Let's raise the sails and catch the wind!

The will of God is not a mysterious set of sealed orders we search for and receive if we happen to hit on the right formula. Rather, the will of God is a relationship with Him in which He discloses His purpose, power, and plan for our lives—and in that order.

God is in search of us! He wants to communicate His ultimate will and His daily guidance. Our intense concern to know His will is because He has chosen and called us. So our discussion of the will of God is in the context of the stunning truth that He wants to reveal it even more than we may want to receive it.

You and I have been wonderfully created. We have been given capacities which correspond directly to the nature of God. We have been endowed with a heart to be persons after His heart. In the biblical sense, our heart is a combination of intellect, emotion, and will. We were meant to be able to think God's thoughts after Him, to receive and express His love, and to will to know and do His will.

He made us that way for a magnificent purpose—to receive His love and to glorify Him. God came in Christ to reveal that purpose and to release power through His death and resurrection so that we could be participants in a relationship of reciprocal love.

Jesus put it clearly. He affirmed the historic

Hebrew statement of our purpose in Deuteronomy 6:5 and Leviticus 19:18, but with a very significant addition: "You shall love the Lord your
God with all your heart, with all your soul, and
will all your mind. This is the first and great com-
mandment. And the second is like it: You shall
love your neighbor as yourself" (Matthew 22:
37-39). A quick check on the Old Testament
rendering reveals that Jesus' addition, or more
accurately His emphasis was the mind. Why did
He say that? If the Hebrew word for "heart"
already implied intellect, emotion, and will, why
stress the mind? It was because Jesus saw the
mind as something more than intellect alone, but
as the port of entry of the Spirit into a human being. The mind is our inner thought, will, and
moral value system.

It is interesting to note that Jesus followed immediately His call to love God with a crucial
question to the Pharisees: "What do you think
about the Christ?" (Matthew 22:42). He knew
that their confused thinking had their wills in
bondage and their value system distorted. With
divine discernment He knew that the conscious
self that is inside humankind was the result of
congealed thought issuing in the will. He also
knew that in Adam's mind the strong thought of
running his own life had thrown the will out of
balance as the servant of his thinking. The
historic fall of man had begun a fracture of the
lines of authority between God, our thought, and
our will. Think of it in military terms as com-
mander-in-chief, general, and lieutenant: God is

our sovereign Commander; our thinking is the general who takes the strategy and works it out in specifics; and the lieutenant is the will, who gets it done by following orders.

The condition of humankind when Jesus came was that the lieutenant was in charge. Willfulness had become the dominant manifestation of the separation of persons from God. That's why so much of Jesus' message deals with the will. William James said that the will was the key to comprehending the life and words of Jesus. Martin Luther focused on this in his benchmark book *The Bondage of the Will.*

I like to call it the "bondage of our false freedom." The will is not free until it is the servant of accomplishing our real purpose. It controls thought rather than implementing the whole person in the actions which will accomplish it. All the talk about the freedom of the will through the ages often misses the mark. In the effort to be sure we maintained the idea of people's freedom to choose to love God, we've taken on the heavy baggage of the idea that, given the possibility, we would choose to respond. That's not the case. Thousands of years of rebellion have thrown our minds out of whack. It is not our natural inclination to love God.

Perhaps it would be better to use the word "libertine" as a description of what we have done with our liberty. "Libertine" means a life of dissoluteness, the lack of resoluteness in moral conduct. Clear thought of our real purpose, willing, and action are in disarray. We are off in all directions rather than unified by a central direction. "But," you say, "what about the moral person who is impeccable in keeping all the rules but has never willed to do the will of God?"

My response is, "What could be more immoral than missing the reason for which we were born?" If our basic purpose is to love the Lord our God, but we don't (by not using our sublime endowments to think, will, and act in response to His love), then the basic reason for our life has been squandered. The lack of resoluteness of will ends up in willfulness. We are like a child in a tantrum of will who can't be reasoned with. The will out of control of thought will turn inward on the self instead of outward to others and to God. We've all been in one of those compulsive states, so we know what that is all about. Some people live that way all the time. One determination after another pulls them in different directions with zeal and passion. The good news, however, is that this is exactly why Christ came.

All this must be said in preparation for a consideration of the wonder of the will. An honest statement about its misuse must not keep us from the available, open secret to the mystery of its real purpose, or the majesty of life when it is liberated from dissoluteness and becomes resolute in obedience to God. How this takes place is the theme of our search. I want us to consider with gratitude what a miracle it is to know the will of God and to receive His guidance in our daily life.

We were wonderfully created to respond to the will of God. We are spiritually endowed with an inner mind, spirit, and soul, which were given to us to receive God's mind, respond to His Spirit, and have our souls prepared for eternity. Our physical brain and nervous system are a magnificent mechanism given to us to accomplish our purpose.

Even an introductory study of the brain startles us with awe and wonder. For example, the orderly way the parts of the brain were created to function in accomplishing the will of God is a cause for adoration. The cerebral cortex of the brain is the control center of many of our conscious or intellectual functions, such as thinking, memory, imagination, fantasizing, dreaming, talking, and association. It also runs the motor activity, physical coordination, and sensory functions, such as sight, hearing, touch, and smell. The limbic system of the brain responds to the orders from the cortex and implements the responses of our emotions and bodies as well as the functions of reflex, appetites, drives, heartbeat, and breathing. It also triggers the supply of hormones in the blood through the hypothalamus, which activates the adrenal and other endocrine glands.

Functioning properly, thought congealed in a decision of the will sets in motion the signals from the cerebral cortex to the limbic and other systems of the nervous system, which produce the emotions, energy, and action needed. As congealed thought, the will has immense power of determination. It was meant to be the servant implementing thought, not the master controlling it. The wonder of the will is that it is capable of making things happen. It is focused attention resulting in desire. The will can become the total person activated to accomplish the magnificent purposes of God in the world. He has a will, and we have been given a will to choose to do His will and cooperate with His guidance. His thoughts can be engendered through our mind into the cerebral cortex of the brain and can be activated in our character and our activity.

The psalmist caught the wonder of our potential. In Psalm 8 he reflects on the excellence of God's creation. He surveys the heavens, the moon and stars, and all that He has ordained. And then, in the context of that wonderment, he suddenly is gripped by the sublime work of the Creator in our human nature: "What is man, that You are mindful of him? And the son of man, that You visit him?" And then he blurts out a startling and stunning realization which sends his mind reeling: "You have made him a little lower than the angels, and You have crowned him with glory and honor. You have made him to have dominion over the works of Your hands; You have put all things under his feet." In rapid-fire order the psalmist lists the extent of that dominion, expressing the excitement of his awe and wonder. Then with humility and delight over God's goodness he concludes with praise: "O Lord, our

Lord, How excellent is Your name in all the earth!''

The psalmist's adoration is where we must begin our discussion of how to know and do God's will for our lives. His discovery is all the more awesome when we realize that the word "angels" in the Hebrew is really *Elohim*, God! That can be interpreted in three ways: God has made us as divine beings, or divine beings like the angels, or a little lower than Himself. Any of the three are motive for unrestrained praise and devotion. We have been deputized by the Lord of all creation to cooperate with Him in the management of our lives and the world. This is our place and function in creation. And to enable us to fulfill our royal status, He has given us the capacity to think His thoughts after Him, to experience and express emotion, and to discern and do His will.

The thing which crowns us with "glory and honor" is the ability to think and choose. An animal has impulses, desires, and inclinations, but it has no *controlling* volitional power. It must obey its desires if nothing external deters it. Training of the habits of the higher species of animals may condition their behavior, but they are not able to discern the value of alternative choices, and so they cannot act on the basis of either purpose or destiny. Only human beings have the endowed capacity of choice. With it we can decide and implement and control our actions. You are aware of that blessing as you read. You can blink your eyes, look away from this page, or move any part of your body. You can also think about alternative choices before you in the management of your life and make decisions about what you are going to do.

So the first step in finding the will of God for our lives is to praise Him for the endowment of the will He has given us. The greatest wonder next to God Himself is our mind. Praise for that gift enables us to begin with the assurance that God has a will and we have a will. The two can become one!

The second step is to acknowledge that we would not desire to know His will for our lives if He were not impinging on our consciousness, seeking to make it known. Revelation of the will of God always begins with Him. If we long to know His will, it is a sure sign that we have been chosen and called to be His persons. He has loved and forgiven us. His Spirit has activated our minds with a desire to be maximum for Him. So if there is a stirring within you to know God's will, stop right now and claim the fact that you are a cherished and beloved person!

There are two Greek nouns used for the will of God in the New Testament. One is *boulēma* and the other is *thelēma*. *Boulēma* is God's immutable, irrevocable will; *thelēma* is His desire for us to experience and live what He has revealed in Christ to be His plan and purpose for all creation.

Acts 2:23,24 is an example of the use of *boulēma*. It is translated into English as "counsel." Jesus, "being delivered by the determined counsel and foreknowledge of God . . .

whom God raised up, having loosed the pains of death, because it was not possible that He should be held by it." The meaning is that the atonement, the resurrection, and Pentecost could not be either detained or deterred. It may have appeared that people caused the cross, but behind their betrayal and belligerence, God's will for the reconciliation of the world was being accomplished. Humanity caused the need for it, but no one could have stopped it.

The other passage in which this strong word *boulēma* is used is Romans 9:19. Paul asks, "For who has resisted His will?" Does that mean we can't say no? What I think is meant is that when we are elected and called into God's will, He also gives us the power to respond. He is the sovereign Lord and Creator of all. Indeed, who can resist Him?

The word *thelēma* is used in other passages about the will of God. It means His strong desire for us. Further, it signifies what God desires (and what is desirable) in fulfilling His intention for us.

Both words are crucial for an understanding of the will of God. His *boulēma* will does not require our cooperation: His *thelēma* will does. One accomplished our salvation; the other calls us into it. Now the two words blend together. Before our conversion, we thought it was all our choice to accept His grace; looking back, we realize that a vital part of His grace was the mysterious, magnetic pull within us to respond. Certainly we could have resisted. But the desire of the almighty, omnipotent God, once it is centered on us in gracious, forgiving love, is difficult to refuse. He calls us to live in the center of His will. Tennyson expressed the mystery: "Our wills are ours, we know not how; our wills are ours to make them Thine." And the Lord's desire is to give us the gift of faith to do nothing less than that.

An appreciation of all that God has done for you and me historically and personally to bring us to this place is absolutely essential. But no person naturally desires God or the knowledge of His will. Notwithstanding the psalmist's exalted declaration of our status, we know what humankind did with its endowments and freedom. The ability to think and make choices was used to rebel against God and seek to be gods rather than only "a little lower than God." That's the pitiful story of man's fall from what he was meant to be. It is called sin. And all aspects of our nature were spoiled by that rebellion, including the will. The psalmist's grand description of us must be understood in the light of the total depravity of human nature because we did not accept the wonder of the will for the purpose for which it was intended —to choose to glorify and love God as the ultimate Lord and Sovereign of our lives.

When you and I were born, we inherited that fallen nature. We were not inherently inclined to love God or seek to do His will. It was by His choice that we were privileged to hear about His love in Christ and what He had done for us in the cross. Our will was not free. It was in bondage to the confused thinking of our mind. Then by sheer grace He came to us. He tracked us down. He persistently worked within us. Through the preaching and teaching of the gospel, or the gracious explanation of a friend whose life in Christ attracted us, we heard the liberating truth of love and forgiveness. Our response was also a gift. We were absolutely incapable of accepting Christ as our Lord and Savior until the gift of faith was given to us. The same Lord who made us a little lower than Himself broke the bonds of self-will and gave us the power to believe and the will to commit our lives to Him. We were born again!

George Matheson discovered the only way the will is liberated from the bondage of willfulness:

> *Make me a captive, Lord,*
> *And then I shall be free;*
> *Force me to render up my sword,*
> *And I shall conqueror be.*
> *I sink in life's alarms*
> *When by myself I stand;*
> *Imprison me within Thine arms,*
> *And strong shall be my hand.*
>
> *My heart is weak and poor*
> *Until it master find;*
> *It has no spring of action sure—*
> *It varies with the wind.*
> *It cannot freely move*
> *Till Thou has wrought its chain;*
> *Enslave it with Thy matchless love,*
> *And deathless it shall reign.*

My will is not my own
Till Thou hast made it Thine;
If it would reach a monarch's throne
It must its crown resign;
It only stands unbent
Amid the clashing strife
When on Thy bosom it has leant
And found in Thee its life.

The first thing we discover is a new set of desires. We sense that our wills are focused on Christ and the desire to know Him better. We are introduced to the Bible and the wisdom it holds for living the new life we have begun. Prayer becomes the lifeline of communication with this new Lord of our lives. Fellowship with other spiritual adventurers becomes the joy of our lives. Worship expresses our feeling of gratitude and praise.

No one is in search of the will of God who has not had this rebirth experience. It is impossible to know or do God's will without it. The will simply does not desire God until God Himself has energized it with the gift of desire, the freedom to respond, and the capacity of making a commitment.

So if you are at the place of wanting to know God's will for the total direction of your life (or in some decision or relationship), you are a chosen, called, loved, and redeemed person. Your will has been set free through your conversion to Christ.

The reason for this emphasis is that in my own

experience and in thousands of conversations with people about the will of God, I have discovered that we think of the will of God as a rigid line on which we must walk rather than as a liberating relationship with Him in which we are privileged to live. We consider the will of God as something He gives us to do, or restrictions He imposes, rather than a life in fellowship with Him.

Surely God does lead us in specifics, but the trap we fall into is that guidance becomes more important than God! We all want to live a full and abundant life. And the seemingly wrong choices we have made have alarmed us about the margin of error we all face. That, and the urging of others that we "find" God's will, puts the burden on us. We try to figure out ways of discovering what He wants us to do. The advice of friends about slick ways of discovering the will of God often becomes confusing. We are told to pray, read the Bible, seek counsel from others, look for signs, and wait for the "right feelings."

All of these are helpful in knowing the will of God, and we will discuss each of them in greater detail, but they were never meant to be our effort to convince God to reluctantly relinquish a clear understanding of what He wants us to do.

God's ultimate will is that we know Him, love Him, glorify Him, and grow in an intimate relationship with Him. I have repeated that for emphasis because it is out of this supreme purpose that specifics are given us. He longs for us to live in close fellowship with Him; He is constantly invading our lives, wanting to guide our every thought, reaction, and decision. He is not aloof, hiding until we say or do the right things to unlock His will. He has come in Jesus Christ to do all that is necessary to transform our minds and liberate our wills to want His will. Now He guides our circumstances to bring us to the place where we will question the direction of our lives and express the need for His help in specific decisions. He has put the thought of His sovereign will into our minds and given us the gift of desire to want to know what is best for our lives. Now with all that preparation, would He withdraw and make the knowledge of His will an obscurity? Hardly!

The other day a man came to see me. He was facing some crucial decisions in his life. "How can I know God's will for my life?" he asked urgently. My temptation was to talk over the issues involved in those decisions, pray with him, and send him on his way. But the convictions I have expressed thus far in this chapter kept me from that. I suspected that God had brought the man to the place of uncertainty about those decisions because He was up to something much more profound than simply giving him detailed directions for several choices he had to make. After he had talked out his dilemma, I reviewed with Him essentially what I've shared with you.

I told him he was a blessed, special person. The fact that he wanted to know God's will was because God had taken the initiative in creating the desire. Then I asked him about his relationship with God. He told me about his conversion to Christ in college and his nominal and rather traditional involvement in the church ever since. Like so many people, he prayed in crises, read the Bible in times of trouble, and was fairly regular in church attendance. He said, "It hit me last Sunday in church that these decisions about my career were very important and that I'd better seek God's guidance. But when I prayed about it, I didn't seem to get a definite answer. That's why I've come to you. How can I be sure of God's will for these decisions?"

He wanted an answer from me right then about what he should do. My response was to share with him the wonder of his capacity to think and will. Then I told him of my own discovery that guidance in specifics comes out of consistent companionship with God. The man had never made a commitment of His will to do God's will. We did that together in the quiet of my study. Fortunately, he had two weeks before his answer about the job opportunity was due. I gave him some passages from the Bible to read and encouraged him to take a definite period each morning and evening to read and pray. His will, now committed and ready, grasped the opportunity. Filled with the enthusiasm of the realization that God was seeking to make His will known, that He had given him the capacity of will to respond, and that he could think God's thoughts and will His will, he left my study with the promise to return the day before his decision was due about the job.

What he said when he returned is the reason I have shared this story. When he entered my study, he was beaming. His whole countenance was radiant and filled with excitement. "I'm so glad that you didn't just help me sort out a decision about that job when I saw you two weeks ago. Instead, you got me back with the Lord again. Decisions like I had to make should have been natural—out of the flow of a consistent companionship with the Lord. It was because I was out of fellowship with Him that the decision became such a big thing. These days of prayer and Bible reading have really helped. But I kept thinking about that statement you quoted to me from the Psalms about how wondrously God has made me with a will and how my conversion released my will to want what God wants for me. It has been exciting to think about my will being a channel of God's will and that the desire to know God's will is because He has been tracking me so that I could listen and receive it. I've made my decision to take the job. But now I see that the decision to stay where I am or move was not the issue. God wanted me—my will—and not just the right decision. Thanks for helping me pull my anchor out of the mud!"

Perhaps you too have an anchor keeping you from full speed ahead. We all have those times when we wring our hands in furtive frustration over knowing the will of God. The recounting of this man's story is not meant to mock our dilemma with a simplistic solution. What I have tried to do, however, is remind myself, and you, that whatever else we say about God's will for our lives, we must begin with these basics. The rest will fall into place after that.

As a start, affirm these great truths:

1. God created us with the wondrous capacity of will.
2. He dealt with the problem of our misuse of our wills in the forgiveness of the cross.
3. Our wills are totally incapable of desiring God's will until they are set free by being born again.
4. We are the chosen, called, beloved of God who have been liberated to will to do His will.
5. The fact that we desire to know His will is because He has singled us out to know it.
6. The purpose of His will is that we know Him, love Him, and grow in an intimate relationship with Him.
7. Specific guidance for daily decisions flows out of a consistent, open, willing relationship with the Lord.

What follows in subsequent chapters will spell this out in greater detail. Now we turn to the artesian well from which all guidance flows—a relationship which allows us to really start living.

2

Now's the Time
to Start Living!

There's a song in the Broadway musical "Pippin" which exposes the contemporary quest to squeeze all of existence into the brief years of this life. It is aptly entitled "No Time At All." The song expresses the panic of growing old and missing the delight of living. Its refrain, "Oh, it's time to start livin'," is catching and lingers on the mind long after your foot stops tapping. Though we might not agree with the values which the lyrics and chorus define as living, we respond to the urgency to start living which they communicate:

> Oh, it's time to start livin',
> Time to take a little from the
>   world we're given;
> Time to take time, 'cause
>   Spring will turn to Fall
> In just no time at all.

This "take time to smell the roses" philosophy is very popular today. It is possible to live so fast and hard that the enjoyment of life is lost. But what does it really mean to start living? The only satisfactory answer must include the present and eternity, or else we feverishly try to cram life into the brief span of this portion of eternity. We are all alive forever. How we live *now* determines how and where we will spend eternity.

God's will is that we really live, both now and forever. Jesus Christ came to live, reveal, and offer us both the abundant life and eternal life. You and I want both! But the second is dependent on the first. In fact, both express the same reality: Life in Christ lived to the fullest both now and beyond the comma in life we call death.

In our search to know and do the will of God, so much is answered by this simple formula: The will of God is that we live to the fullest both in this life and forever in heaven. We have a vague idea of what that means. But we get hassled with the pressures and stresses of life and end so many days feeling that we have existed but have not lived.

So many Christians confess to me that though they feel fairly sure of eternal life, they don't experience what they suspect Jesus meant by the abundant life. Even after conversion, they continue to be wracked with worry, pressured by conflicting demands, and unsatisfied by what their relationships provide or they are able to give to them. As one church member said to me recently, "I'm not as worried about dying in the end as I am about being half-dead right now!"

In a much more profound way than the "Pippin" song expresses, Jesus Christ came and comes to say, "Now's the time to start living!" He would not advise taking from the world we've been given, but He would agree that it is "time to take time" to discover that the will of God for us is life in Him and He in us. Christ is God with us. In the power of the Spirit, He wants to set us free to experience the liberating truth that whatever enables joyous, adventuresome, and courageous living—now and forever—is the will of God. So often we wring our hands in worried search for guidance. Does a choice enable us to grow in Christ and live the abundant life as He lived and taught it? If so, we can press on with the assurance of God's will. If not, it is wasted time ruminating over the possibility. When a choice will stifle Christ's free reign in us or debilitate anyone else's growing relationship with Him, we can be sure it is not the will of God.

Surely there are difficult and painful things we must go through which enable us to grow up as persons. But they are usually clearly defined by obedience to some aspect of discipleship or service which requires faithfulness and follow-through to what Christ has said about losing our lives to find them. When I suggest "Now's the time to start living," that's a part of what I mean. It's time to enter into the full delight of fellowship with Christ, and it's also time to listen carefully to what He said about giving ourselves away lavishly to the needs of others. He has promised to make His home in us. The basic will of God is that we give Him full command and get cracking!

In order to do that, we need three things: an assurance that we belong to Christ and that He lives in us; a total dependence on His shepherding care; and an unreserved commitment to live life to the fullest because we know that we are alive forever.

Jesus promised all three in one of His clearest statements of the will of God. The occasion which prompted His forthright revelation was a conversation with the people who had witnessed the miracle of the feeding of the five thousand. Jesus discerned that they wanted further signs and proofs. What more than the multiplication of the loaves and fishes did they need? Like so many of us who are in a frenzied search for guidance, they wanted further specifics of what they were to do if they were to do the works of God. But Jesus was very direct: "This is the work of God, that you believe in Him whom He sent." That in itself would be an invigorating inventory for us in our search for the will of God. We could occupy a thousand years of life just spelling out the specifics about which there is no need to wonder.

But Jesus went on. He made a bold messianic claim and offered bread that satisfies: "For the bread of God is He who comes down from heaven and gives life to the world." Note the emphasis on life! The people responded, "Lord, give us this bread always."

You and I want to live and not miss the reason we were born. That life is Christ Himself. "I am the bread of life. He who comes to Me shall never hunger, and he who believes in Me shall never thirst." Linger for a moment with me on that momentous statement. Christ is all that we need in every moment of this life so that we can know life at its highest, and then enter into an even greater fullness beyond the grave. This creates the environment in which we can appropriate the specific revelation of the essential will of God which Jesus went on to explain.

Don't miss the uncluttered clarity of this promise: "All that the Father gives Me will come to Me, and the one who comes to Me I will by no means cast out." That is our blessed assurance: We have been elected to belong to Christ. Chosen. Called. The willingness to both hear and respond to that are gifts of the Spirit. We are drawn by the Spirit; our wills are freed by the Spirit, and we are given the settled assurance that we belong to Christ. He will accomplish His work in us. He will never cast us out. He wants us to live even more than we do! Christ's ministry in us is to be sure our wills are liberated and that we have clarity each step of the way regarding what we are to be and do. We are in good hands!

Now here is what He came (and comes) to do so that we can start living: "For I have come down from heaven, not to do My own will, but the will of Him who sent Me." He continues to say those same words in you and me. His indwelling presence molds our wills around His own and guides us in every decision. "This is the will of the Father who sent Me, that of all He has given Me I should lose nothing, but should raise it up at the last day. And this is the will of Him who sent Me, that everyone who sees the Son and believes in Him may have everlasting life."

If all we had to go on in our search for the will of God was that magnificent promise, we would have more than enough. It tells us that God's basic will is our eternal life and that His presence is with us in Christ to get us through the days of this life safely home to heaven. To accomplish that, He went to the cross, rose from the dead, and returned in the power of the Spirit to abide with us and in us forever.

The way He does that is explained in Jesus' promise of the "abundant-life" portion of what is offered to us eternally. He has promised to be our Good Shepherd. We may not like everything about sheep and shepherds, but there is a great deal of similarity in our lack of understanding of the possibilities of the present or the potential of the future which are exemplified by the dependence of the sheep on their shepherd. They are dependent on the shepherd for safety, provision, the path to follow, and where to rest ("lie down in green pastures"). When we echo David's assurance, "The Lord is my Shepherd" (Psalm 23:1), and accept Jesus' "I am the Good Shepherd" (John 10:11), we have the key to the unfolding of God's ultimate and daily will. Again, Jesus states clearly why He came in the incarnation and why He comes to you and me: "I have come that they may have life, and that they may have it more abundantly" (John 10:10). We think of how He accomplished this. He preached the kingdom of God as the secret of the abundant life, God's reign and rule in our minds, giving us new priorities for the focused attention of our wills.

But something more was needed to release the will from the prison of selfishness so that we could will to enjoy the abundance of the kingdom. Calvary. There we experienced a grace which captured our thoughts and flooded our emotions with uncontainable love—for Him, ourselves, and others. The will is now the ready servant of an entirely new purpose. We want to do the will of the One who loved us and gave His life for us.

Knowing and doing the will of God is companionship with the Good Shepherd, Jesus our Lord. As the first truly obedient One in the midst of disobedience, He was the incarnation in the life, death, and resurrection as described in the words of Psalm 40:7,8: "Then I said, 'Behold, I come; in the scroll of the Book it is written of me. I delight to do Your will, O my God.'" The surrender of our wills to Christ means the same thing for us. But that means accepting His willingness to shepherd us each hour, each day.

Martin Luther said that true Christianity consists in personal pronouns. There's a lovely story of a little girl who was fast asleep. When her mother and father checked in on her before they retired, they noticed a serene look on her sleeping face. They also saw that she had one hand clutched around the forefinger of her other hand. At breakfast they asked her why she fell asleep with her forefinger held so tightly.

"Well," she responded, "I repeat the 23rd Psalm before I go to sleep, like you have taught me. I keep saying it over and over again: 'The Lord is my Shepherd.' That's five words. I start counting with my little finger, and when I reach the word 'my,' I'm at my forefinger. I like 'my' best of all! He is *my* Shepherd!"

I hope I never become so sophisticated that when I need clarity about the will of God and guidance for my daily decisions, I am unwilling to grasp my forefinger in personal, childlike assurance! Jesus is *my* Shepherd—He leads me through each step of the abundant, eternal life that He came and comes to provide.

In that context, you and I can claim the promises Christ has made about prayer as the channel through which our wills become attuned to His. "If you abide in Me, and My words abide in you, you will ask what you desire, and it shall be done for you" (John 15:7). We so often leap to the second part of that promise before we meet the qualifying offer of the first part. Jesus and His words must abide in us before we can know what or how to ask. The two-part blessing contains His words, His message available to us to study in the Gospels, and His abiding presence which selects the particular truths we need in any situation and helps us clarify for what we should ask. Abiding in Christ and allowing Him to abide in us is the secret for guidance. It means to make Him our dwelling and to open our minds as His dwelling—to rest, relax, and receive. This habitual abiding, punctuated by consistent times of prayer and study of His Word, will get us ready for the decisions and choices we have to make.

Allow me to share an insight that came to me years ago and has been updated by experiences ever since. One day I was unsure of the will of God in my life. When I prayed, all that came to me were the words, "The restless search for the will of God is a sure sign that you are out of it!" You can imagine that this was not a very comforting answer to my prayer for an undeniable word from the Lord for the decisions I had to make! I mulled the words over for weeks. They led me to a confession that my walk with the Lord had become dull and perfunctory. Several areas of my life were not in good order. I had moved from trusting to strenuous effort to do God's work. My life was more self-effort than a flow of the Lord's grace.

Then when I needed clarity of God's will for my life, I went to Him seeking an answer. But none came—only the insight articulated in the words I just shared with you. Because of the interruption in my communion with the Lord and my resistance to what I already knew was His will for me in other areas, I was not able to convince the Lord to give me what I wanted. He had not closed me out; I had closed Him out.

During the weeks that followed, I got reacquainted with my Shepherd. I allowed Him to take charge of the corridors of my mind which I had closed off. The less I focused on getting the answer to my particular question for immediate guidance, the greater clarity came as to what I should do. The Lord's will for me was to abide, listen, wait—to want *Him* more than His guidance. The Good Shepherd knew the pasture for rest, the flowing stream of spiritual refreshment, and the right path I needed to discern. Out of love for me, He withheld temporarily what I *wanted* in order to give me what I *needed*.

Can you identify with that personal account? Perhaps it speaks to what you're facing right now. The words the Lord gave me, "The restless search for the will of God is a sure sign you're out of it," may sound harsh and insensitive. But let them seep into the tissues of the cortex of your brain. Allow them to focus your thought and then congeal into your will. The One who revealed the essential will of God that we live the abundant life and the eternal life wants to abide in you more deeply than ever before.

It is reassuring to know that the Lord is the same yesterday, today, and tomorrow. It is equally liberating to know that He sees the decisions and choices we are going to have to make. Is it not reasonable to assume that He wants to get us ready? That's His task as *our* Shepherd.

Think of a time when you came up to a really tough decision and knew immediately what you were supposed to do. Remember the delight you felt in being able to be decisive? Chances are very good that the Lord had been getting you ready. Time with Him had clarified your values. His abiding presence had given a healthy sense of self-esteem. You felt good about yourself and your future. There were no complicating areas of resistance to the Lord which drained off your energy and attention, seeking to interpose themselves as the issue of your present choice. Your mind was free of guilt over unconfessed sins. Remember Amos's question: "Can two walk together, unless they are agreed?" (Amos 3:3). Abiding with Christ had surfaced those areas of disagreement, and they had been resolved with confession and forgiveness. You felt free, assured, in tune with the Lord, and the act of will crystallizing your thought seemed obvious. What in other times would have been a source of turmoil in seeking the Lord's will was obviously the way to go, and you exercised your will with freedom and assurance.

Is it too much to expect that this is the way the Shepherd wants us to live consistently?

Unless I miss my guess, you are probably thinking, "Yes, but some things are more difficult than others. There are times when I'm really up against it and don't know God's will for my life."

But is anything too big for the Lord? Does He will the anguished times of uncertainty? He has all power in heaven and earth! The long period we endure wrestling is often caused by the difficulty of bringing our wills into alignment with His, rather than by His reluctance to show us the way.

A woman said to me, "I don't know what God is waiting for! It has taken Him so long to make His will plain in this situation. I'm ready; I only wish He were!"

Was He not ready? Did He not know the resolution of the problem in that situation? Or was He waiting for this woman to be made ready? In fact, that was exactly the case. The timing was not right; she was running ahead of the Lord. When He cooled her heels and got her in harmony with His abiding presence, she saw the answer which had been waiting there all along!

The will of the Lord that we should live—now and forever—is perfectly congruent with the three basic desires that He has placed in us. We all want to be maximum in the realization of our potential; we all quest to enjoy the years of our life to the fullest; and we all long for the assurance that this life is but a brief part of eternity for us. The zest for life is the endowment of the Lord of all life.

That's why Jesus' statement of the will of God is so powerful: It fulfills God's intention and our inclination. The Apostle John was moved to stunning rhetoric about that wondrous blend of man's need and God's provision: "In Him was life, and the life was the light of men .... As many as received Him, to them He gave the right to become children of God, even those who believe in His name; who were born, not of blood, nor of the will of the flesh, nor of the will of man, but of God" (John 1:4,12,13).

Life as Christ lived it and life as He lives it in us is the only way to satisfy our real desires and His demands. He is God's will for us. That will is perfect in that it ensures our potential, accomplishes our purpose, and assures us of perpetuity.

Our longing for perfection can be met only as

the One who is perfect takes up residence in us. The word "perfect" in the Greek means end or goal. Christ dwelling in us is the Maximizer of all our potential. As the Wisdom of God, He inspires our thinking. As the Power of God, He infuses us with the willing, engendering strength to seek and want to follow His guidance. The Good Shepherd's ministry in our lives is to help us face the opportunities and challenges of life on His power. And nothing is impossible for Him!

Next consider our desire to know and accomplish our purpose. Again Christ is our Guide. He focuses for us our ultimate purpose to be His person and to glorify Him in all that we do. His message charts the way, showing us how to love others and give ourselves away in service. The needs of people and their suffering become our deep concern. Their longing to live abundantly becomes the motive of sharing what Christ has meant to us. And moment-by-moment, daily guidance is given by His abiding, indwelling presence. Paul expressed the basic purpose for which we were born: "Let this mind be in you which was also in Christ Jesus" (Philippians 2:5). With that gift, our purpose and all our plans to reach it will be sorted out and sifted and made one with the Lord's will.

And finally, our fear of death and the desperate need of an assurance of perpetuity are more than satisfied in the risen Christ. He defeated the powers of death and rose from the grave. Because He lives, we live also—forever. Death for you and me is behind us. It occurred when we surrendered our lives—mind, emotion, will, and body—to the Lord. Our funeral, celebrating the death of willfulness, was also the joyous day of our rebirth. By the will of the Lord and not our own strength, "You He *made alive,* who were dead in trespasses and sins" (Ephesians 2:1). And now we are free to live life—the resurrected life—by the power of the Lord within us.

Thus we can see how perfectly Christ fulfilled His task and continues to fulfill it in us today. Nothing God wants or we need has been left out. Our only challenge is to accept it and begin living in it. And He even provides that! Now's the time to start living—indeed. In the will of the Lord!

3

Surrender to Win

I was startled recently by an advertisement for *Fortune* Magazine. It featured an infant in diapers looking you straight in the eye with a childlike directness and inquisitiveness. The line at the top of the picture was an attention-getter: "We're all created equal. After that, baby, you're on your own." That prompted me to read the copy promoting the magazine!

"Nobody's going to hand you success on a silver platter. If you want to make it, you'll have to make it on your own—your own drive, your own guts, your own energy, your own ambition.

"Yes, ambition. You don't have to hide it anymore. Society's decided that now it's o.k. to be up-front about the drive for success. Isn't that what the fast track is all about?

"If you're one of the fast-track people, your business reading starts with *Fortune.*"

What do you think about that? I've thought a

lot about it! I'm not one to knock either success or ambition, and least of all good hard work. But it's the saying at the top of the ad that rumbles in my soul. Is it true that we're all created equal, or that we're created with an equal opportunity to use our gifts and talents? And the statement that after birth we're on our own is a bit simplistic. For a Christian, it's untrue.

Ad writers are not usually theologians or philosophers, but many of them know human nature very well. That's why they are able to catch our attention. They touch the raw nerve of our deep desires.

But I've got to be honest: The reason the ad got my attention is that it expresses an attitude which we Christians sometimes communicate to people who make a start in the new life in Christ. Let me reword it to express what we imply to many who have had an authentic beginning experience by commiting their wills to the Lord: "After rebirth, saint, you're on your own!"

It's what happens to us after we take seriously the awesome promises Jesus made to us in the previous chapter that counts. And His secret is: Surrender to win!

Not *give up*, but *give in*. In every situation there is a maximum alternative which He wants to give us. Our problem is that we struggle to do it our own way, without asking for His help.

One of the slogans of my church's television ministry is "Turn your struggles into stepping-stones." That's not just a trite alliteration. I really mean it. I believe it can happen. But most of our struggles are in trying to make it on our own. I get hundreds of letters every day from Christians who are struggling, and the struggle usually involves a reluctance to entrust our relationships, responsibilities, problems, and potentials to the Lord. It is usually only after a long struggle of self-effort that we cry out, "Lord, help me!" or "I give up!"

Don't get the idea that I'm suggesting sitting around doing nothing, waiting for the Lord to do everything for us. What I am advocating is a willing will that yields all our affairs to the Lord's thought-conditioning and will-conforming inspiration.

The testimony of Christians through the ages is that there is a magic moment in their problems when they surrender them to the Lord. Their vision is brightened, their perception of possibilities enlarged, and their insight and strength increased. The Lord has power to release, people to deploy to help us, and doors to open with new solutions that we never dreamed possible.

The will is the key. James Jauncy said, "The Lord will not cross the picket line of the will." I believe that's true. But I also believe that He's at work trying to convince us to open the picket line and invite Him into the complexities and concerns we are confronting.

If we agree that the will is congealed thought refined to the hot metal of desire, then the Lord has a divine-sized task ahead with all of us. And if it is true that the will is the servant of the thinking portion of our brains, then the transformation of our presuppositions, values, goals, and beliefs has to be a reformation of those around His mind. That's what maturing in the Christian life is all about.

This is the reason Jesus spent so much time talking about the will. He knew us well. He knew that the will was like a thermostat which, when opened by the warmth of His love, could release the flow of obedient discipleship. He not only came to tell us, "Now's the time to start living," but He gave us concrete teaching, parables, and a powerful prayer to help us grow in discipleship. We're not on our own after rebirth! The Lord wants to finish what He's begun. He is with us in the power of the Holy Spirit.

Our biggest struggles are probably the result of His invasion into our minds. He's at work penetrating into our thinking and willing, but always with empathy and sensitivity. He's never over/against us. He is one with us in our needs and wants to help us let go of our willful control so that the floodgates can be opened to the inrush of His immeasurable power.

Norman Rockwell has given us unforgettable paintings which grab our heartstrings and draw us into the frame of the picture. The secret of doing that was taught him by his teacher, Thomas Fogarty. "Step over the frame, Norman," he urged, "over the frame and live in the picture."

Jesus did that in a sublime way. He stepped into the drama of life and taught us how to release our wills.

In the Sermon on the Mount, Jesus gave us the

Magna Charta of the kingdom of God. In it He also taught us how to pray about our wills. The Lord's Prayer, perhaps more properly called the Disciple's Prayer, outlines how His followers can realize the power of prayer. He shows us that prayer for God's kingdom and His will are inseparably linked. The reign and rule of God in our minds, our lives, our relationships, and our society is the focus of praying for the will of God. To ask for God's kingdom to come is a daring prayer. It is to want the full control of His sovereignty in our lives and all our affairs. And He's more ready to give than we are to ask. In fact, as we've discussed, the desire is His gift. And so is the freedom to pray, "Your will be done on earth, as it is in heaven."

I've pondered that "as it is in heaven" for many years. What's your picture of heaven? Mine is greatly enriched by John's vision in the Book of Revelation. The thing which always impresses me about his inspired glimpses of heaven is that there is a willing community of all the elders, angels, archangels, and cherubim in praise and adoration to the Lord. They are of one mind and spirit about the plan and purpose of the Lord and are participants in His strategy for the culmination of history, the return of Christ, and the final victory.

Adding to that biblical vision is my foretaste of heaven in those times when I've been completely surrendered and open to the will of God. My will, for a time, seemed to be congruent and consistent with His, and the joy which surged through my being was sublime. Now multiply that with the factor of the glory of the Lord, and you have an inkling of what heaven will be like. The key words of the elders around the throne are, "Hallelujah and amen!" Praise God and so be it.

Now back down to earth! Back to your life and mine. Our families. Marriages. Singleness. Jobs and the scramble for a living. Difficult people and impossible situations. A long way from heaven, you say! But the distance from where we are to where the Lord is willing to take us is measured by our willingness to pray, "Your will be done on earth, as it is in heaven." Often crises prompt us to pray it. The goal is to make it as natural as breathing and as expected as tomorrow's sunrise.

The issue is that just as the essential will of the Lord is that we live abundantly and eternally, so too His will for all our relationships and responsibilities is that they be filled with His love and power. The kingdom must reign in us as persons before there's any effectiveness in praying for it in our affairs.

Prayer for the knowledge of what the Lord wills is the powerful prelude to asking that His will be done. That means sincerely asking what He wants us to be and do in the situations which concern us. Often the question helps, "If I loved God with all my heart and wanted His best, regardless of the cost to me, what would I do?" In the same Sermon on the Mount in which we are admonished to pray that God's will be done, we are given some clear promises and clarifications of what are the bases of doing that will. In the Beatitudes, Jesus describes true joyousness or blessedness as confessing our need; feeling grief over what we and others have done with the gift of life; being meek, completely leadable and moldable; desiring rightness with God and His righteousness in all of life; expressing to others the lovingkindness and mercy we've experienced; wanting God, with purity of heart, more than anything or anyone else; and initiating the peace He has established in our hearts between us and others, between the people of our lives, and in the conflicts of the world in which we live. That's enough, for openers, on what the Lord's will surely is in areas where we long for specific guidance.

But Jesus goes on. Being the salt of the earth is also part of God's will. We are meant to bring zest in life's dullness, preservation of the kingdom's goals, savor with spontaneity and sparkle. Consider carefully what it would mean to be the light of the world in your home, on the job, or with your friends. We can be sure that the will of the Lord involves being a contagious witness to what He means to us. We are assigned also the task of understanding and communicating the light of His truth in the darkness of distorted values and conflicts in and between people. That's enough to keep us busy the rest of our lives!

Now Jesus gets down to the heart of the matter. The heart of the issue is obedience to what we know of God's will. Isaiah 29:13 was on Jesus' mind as He confronted the hardness of the hearts of His people: "Inasmuch as these people draw near to Me with their mouths and honor Me with their lips, but have removed their hearts far from Me . . . ." But then Isaiah goes on to promise "a marvelous work and a wonder" that shall be done—a prediction of the Messiah's coming. And His message and life were targeted for the transformation of the heart—the mind, emotions, and will.

The Lord went on in the Sermon on the Mount to spell out His fulfillment of the Ten Commandments in calling for a decision of the will to live them in a much more profound way. Here again we see how the Lord emphasized the will. Beliefs had become fragmented from the volitional power of the brain. The last stage in thinking—decision and desire to act—had been omitted. The endowed capacity of the will became immobilized because of lack of positive use. This volitional power actually was used *against* doing God's commandments instead of obeying them.

But because Christ knew that the Spirit of the Lord was upon Him "to proclaim liberty to the captives" (Isaiah 61:1,2), He pressed on to give guidance to those who had been released by His love to want to hear Him gladly. The Sermon on the Mount makes little sense and is a collection of pious sayings until the Spirit gives the liberating gift in the brain to will to trigger into action the auditory nerve and the awesome mechanism of hearing and registering truth. The volitional part of us has the capacity to implement thought, but also to impair the capacity to receive it.

To those given the will to hear, Jesus gave the startling essentials of His way of life for them. They were to go the second mile, turn their cheeks when insulted, love people who were classified as enemies, and give themselves away without concern for recognition.

Prayer was to be conversation with God in the "secret place," not to impress others, but to allow Him to impress His will on their minds. He would hear and guide them. And the only line in His model prayer which He explained was that we cannot receive forgiveness unless we give it to others.

The prayer of the kingdom people was to ask, seek, and knock. Ask for the Lord's will, seek what that is, and knock with boldness, knowing that the door of opportunity of doing it will be opened.

Worry and anxiety are cut at their taproot by seeking first the kingdom of God and His righteousness. The one concern which heals all lesser concerns is the concern to put God first in our lives.

And then all of this magnificent guidance for living is nailed down by a clear declaration that "Not everyone who says to Me, 'Lord, Lord,' shall enter the kingdom of heaven, but he who does the will of My Father in heaven." With messianic authority He had just explained the ramifications of that will. Now He called for the final stage in comprehension—the decision of the will to live them.

The parable of the two builders seals the emphasis. One built on sand, the other on rock. The rains, floods, and wind destroyed the first, but the other was immovable. The foolish builder heard but did not will to act; the wise builder heard and willed to implement the truth.

The same is true for you and me. This brief review of the Lord's teaching from the Mount in Galilee above the Sea spells out so clearly what it means to pray that God's will be done on earth as it is in heaven. It would be a taste of heaven for us and the people around us if we willed to live it. A multitude of questions about doing the will of God are answered. If we started with the Sermon on the Mount and willed to live its demanding challenges, we would be well on the way; secondary questions about specifics would follow naturally.

This was the life-conviction of Dr. Henrietta Mears, the distinguished Director of Christian Education for so many years at the Hollywood Presbyterian Church. She led thousands of young people to Christ. Her ministry with college students is a benchmark for evangelism among collegians. Hundreds of them became clergy and church leaders. Several significant movements which are impacting the nation today were begun under her influence. The persistent question asked of her by people was how to find God's will for their lives. She was very direct in dispelling the mystery: "Will is the whole man active. I cannot give up my will; I must exercise it. I must will to obey. When God gives a command or a vision of truth, it is never a question of what He will

do, but of what we will do. To be successful in
God's work is to fall in line and do it His way."

That's quite a challenge! In the light of it, you
and I should dare to trust the vision and direction
we already have, and then act on it. That's the
secret of receiving more guidance. God unfolds
His will to those who have acted on what He has
already revealed. That's what Jesus told the
Jews who marveled at His teaching: "How does
this Man know letters, having never studied?"
The question brought forth another affirmation
of the importance of being willing: "If anyone
wants to do His will, he shall know concerning
the doctrine, whether it is from God or whether I
speak on my own authority." The implication for
us is that when we want God's will, we shall
know as much as we are willing to act on today.
More will come when that is done.

The key which unlocks the clarity of His will is
surrender. Our "need" always to be in control is
a misuse of our will. It is defensive thought issuing in a tenacious grip on life, people, and situations. But here again, the Lord does not attack
our imperiousness. Instead, He creates the
thought in us that we are at the end of our own
resources and ability, and that He is willing to
help us. What seems to be a desperate relinquishment is really an unbinding of our volition
to allow Him to love us by doing for us what we
could not do ourselves. It isn't that the Lord
defeats our wills; He sets us free. And in the act
of surrender, we win. A bit of heaven happens!

4

The Cross and Our Will

At this point I am aware of a growing uneasiness inside. You may be feeling it too. We've made some bold statements about the Lord's will and His power to free us to want what He wants for us. That may imply that knowing and doing the will of God are easy. He congeals our thoughts about what we are to do and energizes our wills as the final stage of that prayerful thinking, and off we go to do what He wants!

Is it always that pat for you? It's not for me! There are times when Bible study and prayer implant some thoughts of the will of God for me which put an exorbitantly high price tag on the cost of discipleship.

We pray about the Lord's will for a broken relationship, when suddenly we realize that being faithful demands going to the person in question and confessing our part in the conflict. That means giving up the delicious feeling that we are completely right and that we are the misused and misunderstood person in the breakdown of communication.

We talk to God about someone who has hurt or harmed us, and the thought that we should go and forgive her or him becomes a conviction of the will. But then we protest, "Why should I be the one to forgive? I'm the one who should be asked for forgiveness!" We resist the guidance.

We face difficult decisions about the implementation of the gospel in gray areas of compromise in our employment. The more we pray about it, the more we know what we must do in order to live out our faith. The truth forms into a desire to do it, but we know that it will mean swimming upstream against the currents of cultural values. Now our wills want two things: what the Lord has guided, and what will avoid conflict and rejection.

We pray about our marriages. We ask for God's will for a deeper love, communication, and mutually satisfying lifestyle. The idea hits us of what we could do to open the way for really cherishing each other and enjoying the days we have together. We know what to do, but we put off doing the things which will make a difference. We live with the low-grade fever of blandness because we are unwilling to put into action the costly changes of our habits or selfish demands.

We know that we have been given the answer to life's deepest needs and most urgent questions in our faith in Christ. We become alarmed by the number of our friends and acquaintances who do not know Christ and without Him are not living abundantly now and will not live forever. That leads us to pray about our silence and lack of contagious witness. The Lord shows us some practical ways of caring about the people for whom we have concern, and when we have earned the right to be heard in sharing our faith, He shows us how to talk about what He means to us. But that means giving up our reserve and taking on more involvement for follow-through than we think we may want to give.

Some issues in our society become clear. The more we pray about them, the more we know what a Christian ought to do. More cowards than crusaders or reformers, we wrestle with the mandates of our faith. Our minds come to clear conclusions which must be implemented about the hungry, the poor, and the need for witness in politics. We know what we are called to do, but we recoil at the expenditure of time and energy in this endless battle for truth.

In the area of finances, we pray for the Lord's will in times of crisis. He steps in and extricates us from the problem. Then in our prayers, the question forms: Have I ever trusted the Lord with the complete management of my resources? Why is the clear biblical mandate of tithing such a hassle to me? We reflect on the oft-quoted passage of God loving a joyous giver. (The word in Greek actually means "hilarious.") The unsettling thought begins to grow: Why not enter into partnership with the Lord in our finances and make Him the Senior Partner in decisions about everything—not only what we give but what we spend for our own comfort? Suddenly we realize that our independent, unguided decisions about our expenditures have precluded courageous giving to the needs of others, the mission of the church, and special causes that the Lord lays on our hearts.

In an even deeper dimension, some are wondering about their life's work. Many of you who read this are frustrated with your jobs and wish you could do something else. Some pray asking for God's will. Often the answer comes, "What would you like to do with your life?" We taste the freedom of being able to think about another job or profession or position where we could accomplish our life goals more creatively and our faith more adventuresomely. But it may mean sacrifice. Are we sure it would work? The will is ready, but it is confused and given mixed signals by our thoughts of fear and caution. Most of us choose our pain. The limitations of what we are doing are more sure than the uncertainty of the future out of the comfort of the rut.

By this time you're probably saying, "Okay, I've got the point!" My prayer is that the above illustrations of painful choices will have touched some of the raw nerves in you and that you will focus on the personal areas where you are being pressed out onto the edge of living your faith in a costly way.

They bring us to the cross. When Jesus called us to deny ourselves and take up our cross, He called for an exercise of the will which is very demanding. To understand and be willing to respond, we need to consider His cross, our essential cross, and our daily crosses. James Jauncy said, "Guidance is highly consecrated and sanctified thinking."*

The cross of Christ must be the basis of that thinking if our wills are to be activated to accept our cross. It is helpful to remember that the incarnate Christ was both God and man. He came to reveal what God is like as well as what we are meant to be. There was a perfect union of the human and divine. He was the Mediator between us and God, and therefore He revealed the mind of the Creator. But He also assumed our humanity so that He could return us to the status of grace for which we were created. Though the Spirit of God was uniquely upon Him, He submitted to our physical frailties and limitations. He also had a mind which included the faculty of will. All through His life He prayed for the will of God to be done. Christ is both the perfect revelation of complete obedience to God's will and the One whose obedience makes possible the liberation of our volitional gift.

All through the later part of His ministry, He spoke of His death as the reason He was born. As soon as His disciples recognized Him as the Christ, He began to teach them about His impending cross. In spite of their fear and efforts to dissuade Him, He set His face steadfastly toward

*James Jauncy, *Guidance By God* (Grand Rapids: Zondervan, 1969), p. 61.

Jerusalem with determination of will. He knew that He was to be the sacrifice for the sins of the whole world. His mind was filled with the messianic predictions and prophecies of the prophets of the Old Testament. He knew He was the Lamb of God sent for the accomplishment of a cosmic atonement. The cross was in the heart of God before it was on Calvary. And Jesus had come from the heart of God. His will was to do the will of the Father who sent Him.

The Scriptures are very honest about the agony of will that Jesus went through both before and during His death on the cross. Don't forget His humanity as well as His divinity. As representative man, He sweated blood in the exercizing of His will. We are told that in Gethsemane He "fell on His face and prayed, 'O My Father, if it is possible, let this cup pass from Me; nevertheless, not as I will but as You will' " (Matthew 26:39). That shows us the startling, and ultimately comforting, truth that Jesus as Son of man had taken on Himself the burden of the release of our crippled wills. He knew that he had to go to Calvary, but if there could have been a different way than the anguish of the cross, He would have humanly desired it. The key word on which the redemption of the world was held in balance was "nevertheless." Now the Son of God, Immanuel, God with us, made the choice: "Not as I will but as You will." He went on to be the ransom for our sins, the One who took our sentence and paid the price for man's sin and rebellion before that awesome cross and ever since. He fulfilled the judgment of God on our sin and established in history the eternal basis of our knowledge and experience of God's grace.

And the wonder of it all is that through His cross all facets of our humanity have been redeemed and reconciled to God, including the function of our brain which we call the will.

It was only after the cross, the resurrection, and the return of Christ in the power of the Spirit that the disciples could understand and appropriate what He had said about taking up their cross. Then, under His inspiration and indwelling initiative, they discovered that they had a new power. They could think clearly, feel passionately what those thoughts engendered, and want to do His will faithfully. The fact that they too had a cross made sense. They were not to repeat the atonement, but to live and communicate its grace, hope, and freedom. A new humanity of willing people had been born!

Today, the cross means dying to ourselves and the will to run our own lives. It is accepting the fact that we cannot save ourselves. The love revealed in Christ's cross motivates us to accept ourselves as loved to the uttermost. Suddenly we are possessed with entirely new thoughts about His purpose and our plans; we want to live for the One who gave Himself for us. Praise and thanksgiving result in a strange new capacity we never knew before: willingness. We want to follow our Savior and do what He commands.

That brings us to our daily cross. That's simply our willingness applied to the decisions of each day. It also involves some of those sticky issues I listed at the beginning of this chapter.

In many of them we are tempted to pray, "O my Lord, if it is possible, let this cup pass from me." We want to escape the painful choice of obeying. We long to retreat from the responsibility that has been given us. And we wish that Jesus had been a little less clear about the character and behavior He wants in His disciples. Our longing is for the comfort of the equivocation, "If I only knew what He wanted me to do, I'd do it." We already know more than we wish we knew about what faithfulness requires.

Then the compelling word "nevertheless" comes to our mind. We remember the One who said it for us at the ultimate crisis of history. It is then that we are able to say it, not with dutiful resignation but with triumphant expectation. The risen Christ shows us that His will is not against ours; it is infinitely better than ours. With that we are able to say, "Not my will based on my limited perception, but Your will enabled by Your unlimited power!"

We could end this portion of our discussion on that upbeat note. You and I probably agree that what we've said should be more than enough to motivate us to make those tough decisions. We know what we have to do to be faithful disciples.

But whenever I get to this point in talking about the cross and the Lord's will with an individual or group, the question is sure to arise, "What about Satan's power to keep us from knowing and doing the will of God?"

Certainly the last thing Satan wanted was Christ's cross. And he would like to dissuade us from taking up our own cross. Christ's ministry was a constant battle with Satan and the forces of evil. When Peter tried to dissuade Christ from His commitment to the cross, the Lord said, "Get behind me, Satan!" He knew the disciple was an unknowing agent of satanic influence. Christ came to do battle with Satan's bondage of His people. He engaged him in conflict at every stage of His ministry. Many of the scribes and Pharisees who confronted the Lord exemplified the bondage of Satan over the human will. Some even went so far as to suggest that the power in Christ was Satan. The skirmishes led to the final battles in Gethsemane and on Calvary. And Christ won! The resurrection was the undeniable validation of His atoning death.

As Christians we have some compelling convictions to sustain us. Our wills are no longer in bondage to Satan. Christ has set us free. The fact of the cross and the liberating work of His Spirit in us have transformed us from the kingdom of darkness to the kingdom of light. We belong to Christ, and that will never change. As chosen and called persons, we have been sealed against satanic possession.

And yet, we've all known Christians who do many hurtful and sometimes destructive things. Right now I have a man on my mind and in my prayers almost hourly. He is a converted, born-again believer in Christ. However, in the past few months he has been bent on self-destruction in his involvement with his secretary, his determination to end his marriage, his violent, physically abusive behavior to his family, and his totally irrational behavior. Christian psychological counseling has exposed some of his unmet emotional needs which have caused his unbridled rage, but insight has not deterred his will to tear down the structure of his life and destroy the people he has loved.

Friends who try to analyze what's happening to this man wonder if he was ever truly converted, if he ever had an authentic rebirth experience. Some say he is Satan-possessed, and others have offered to exorcize him of the demons.

The frightening and deeper truth is exposed in the long process by which he got to where he is. He believes in Christ, but had drifted from daily communion with Him and obedience to His guidance. His thoughts about Christ and His kingdom seldom congealed into volitional decisions and actions. Because his will was not strengthened by daily exercise, it was underdeveloped, like muscles which become flabby. His present willfulness is an expression of that. His will is fragmented from thought and reason. He has become a shooting target for satanic influence.

As I pray for my friend, I think of Jesus' words to Simon Peter during His final days in Jerusalem: "Simon, Simon! Indeed, Satan has asked for you, that he may sift you as wheat. But I have prayed for you, that your faith should not fail;

and when you have returned to Me, strengthen your brethren."

I know that this man will not be lost. When I saw him recently, I felt the first evidence of a desire to return to fellowship with the Lord to whom He belongs. In our conversation I listened, confronted, and shared Christ's love. I never felt more acutely the need for Christ's infilling invasion into a human mind to activate a paralyzed will. When I suggested the need to accept that gift before he sorted out all the other issues, his response was that he was willing to be made willing. That's enough for starters. The road ahead will not be easy, but he's on the way.

That extreme illustration focuses the issue. A will which is misused will eventually turn against us. The entertaining of uncreative thought will feed the will with distorted data. Eventually we willfully do a very stupid or destructive thing. Meanness is the will enacting mean thoughts. Selfishness is the outgrowth of pride. Envy is the insecurity of an unstable state of grace. Gossip is a sure sign of lack of love for ourselves as unique and special. Combative competition is caused by our lack of clear understanding of what *we* were meant to be and do.

When we drift into an ever-increasing preoccupation with the wrong kind of thinking, we end up having used our wills so consistently for the wrong things that we find it difficult to respond to the implications of the cross for the decisions we need to make and the actions we need to take. We become our own worst enemy. Every positive thought is countered by a negative one. We think we know what we should do, but the alternatives keep us from doing anything.

The only way back to clarity of thought and resoluteness of will is to begin with the simplest, most basic things. Tell the Lord what has happened and that you want to make a new start. He has not let you go; the very reason for the desire is His grasp on your life. Then think through one basic thing each day that faithfulness to Christ creates a desire to do. Do it at all costs! Your thinking-willing mechanism will grow stronger. And when you are ready, He will create the desire to do some adventuresome things for His glory where only His power could pull them off.

We are the Lord's people. He will not forget or forsake us. He is greater than the force of evil. And He has given us a powerful defense: His Name! The name of Jesus Christ overcomes Satan's influence. In His name we can say, "Get behind me, Satan!" Saying that and meaning it is a great act of will. It means that we have been blessed with the Spirit's freedom to want to know and do the Lord's will.

Now we can think joyfully of the possibilities ahead spelled out by Christ's cross and our own. He will make it plain and fire up our will to obey.

The great English poet William Cowper was often seized by great moments of doubt and despair. One night he had an urgent impulse to drown himself in the River Thames. He got a cab and told the driver to take him to the river. As they drove, a dense fog fell and kept the cabman from finding the river. After driving around in confusion, the cabbie let Cowper out on the street. Cowper stumbled about and suddenly found himself on his own doorstep. Realizing that he had been saved from killing himself, he went inside and wrote the words to "Light Shining Out of Darkness." He was convinced that it was God who had caused the fog to appear and save his life.

> God moves in a mysterious way
>   His wonders to perform;
> He plants His footsteps in the sea,
>   And rides upon the storm.
>
> Deep in unfathomable mines
>   Of never-failing skill,
> He treasures up His bright designs,
>   And works His sovereign will.
>
> Ye fearful saints, fresh courage take;
>   The clouds ye so much dread
> Are big with mercy, and shall break
>   In blessing on your head.

5

The Power to
Do the Lord's Will

I am startled each time I read the opening
sentence of the Book of Acts. It stretches my mind
beyond the Gospels as the extent of what Jesus
Christ revealed about the will of God. Luke, the
author, knew that the incarnation in the life and
ministry of Jesus of Nazareth was only the beginning. Without the atoning cross and the power of
the resurrection, there would have been no foundation for knowing God's will for our lives. "The
former account I made, O Theophilus, of all that
Jesus *began* both to do and teach" (Acts 1:1).

It's that word *began* that always catches my
attention. In our search for the will of the Lord,
we have only begun when we have considered
what Jesus said and did during His earthly
ministry. A study of what He continued to do and
teach in and through His followers in the Book of
Acts is absolutely necessary for knowing and doing His will.

We are like the disciples. After we've beheld the glory of what Christ did for us, we still are not able to do His will. When we read the record of their lives after the resurrection, we are amazed. Some doubted, others questioned, and all felt both inept and impotent to do anything about it. The first chapter of the Book of Acts also depicts our lives. After all that Jesus had done, they asked, "Will You at this time restore the kingdom to Israel?" (Acts 1:6). In a sense they were saying, "Lord, we became Your disciples because we thought You were going to bring Israel back to the glory of the Davidic kingdom. We appreciate what You did in the cross and the resurrection, but when are You going to be concerned about our agenda?" They were looking back; the risen Christ was looking forward. Something much more wonderful than David's kingdom was about to be given. It would happen in them and between them, and the world would be changed. "It is not for you to know times or seasons, which the Father has put in His own authority. But you shall receive power when the Holy Spirit has come upon you; and you shall be witnesses to Me in Jerusalem, and in all Judea and Samaria, and to the end of the earth" (Acts 1:7,8).

What Jesus had *begun* would be continued. The revelation of the Lord's will would be exposed in what He would *continue* to do when He came within His followers and gave them enabling power.

The life and message of Jesus Christ brings us to the edge of knowing what we should be and do, but we seem to lack the power to actually do it; our wills seem more blocked than before. Our minds have responded to the magnificent truth that Jesus taught and lived. We have new priorities. But we still have no power to will to act.

In the last chapter I tried to be specific about the mandates of the kingdom of God. Did that leave you a bit frustrated? I hope so. For that prepares us for what Jesus Christ is continuing to do today.

F.B. Meyer, the incisive biblical expositer of another generation, illustrates this feeling in an incident when he was crossing the Irish Channel. It was a dark, starless night.

"I stood on the deck by the captain and asked him, 'How do you know Holyhead Harbor on so dark a night as this?' He said, 'You see those three lights? Those three lights must line up behind each other as one, and when we see them so united, we know the exact position of the harbor's mouth.' "

Meyer spells out the implication. "When we want to know God's will, there are three things which always concur—the inward impulse, the Word of God, and the trend of circumstances. God in the heart, impelling you forward; God in the Book, collaborating whatever He says in the heart; and God in circumstances. Never start until all three things agree."

At this point you and I have two of those lights in line. We have the inclination, or we wouldn't be spending this time in quest of the Lord's will. We also have the clear light of the example and mighty acts of the Word Incarnate. Now we need the third light of seeing what the Lord is doing in our circumstances and what He wants us to do to cooperate with Him in the accomplishment of His will. All three lights are the gift of Pentecost. The infilling of the Spirit creates the impulse, the inspiration, and the insight we need. The indwelling Lord creates the desire to do His will, convinces us of our new life in Him, and clarifies what we are to do in specific circumstances.

That's exactly what happened to Christ's followers when He baptized them with His Spirit in the Upper Room at Pentecost. He came in what they described as a mighty wind, fire, and a new ability to praise Him and communicate His love to others. The wind was a familiar way of describing the Spirit of God for those Hebrews. *Ruach*, the breath of God, was moving mightily. It started the greatest movement of history—the church. The fire which hovered over their heads entered their hearts—mind, emotions, and will. It refined and purified. The fire of the Spirit burned out the chaff of confused thinking and befuddled reservations. It refined their thinking about the cross, resurrection, and ascension of Jesus. He was who He had said He was: Messiah, Immanuel, the Power of God. As a result of the centering fire they felt a compelling desire to love, serve, and share Him. The volitional capacity of their brains was healed, energized, and empowered. They could not contain their praise! And its contagious glow was so attractive that they were given a receptive hearing for their exciting message of what Jesus Christ meant to them.

The Book of Acts, which records what the Lord said and did through them, is a pulsating account of how you and I were meant to live. The title sometimes used is "The Acts of the Apostles," and that stirs us to action. It should more accurately be called "The Acts of the Holy Spirit," and that opens us to the immense possibility of the same courageous, bold, and daring Christianity today.

The crucial thing for me which the "Acts of the Holy Spirit" teaches about the Lord's will is that He moved both within and ahead of those early Christians. He was the Master Strategist. As they prayed, kept in close fellowship with one another, and worshiped together, they were pulled on into the next step of His strategy. They were breathless constantly in their effort to sort out and explain the meaning of what He had done through them.

A key verse which explains what was happening is a promise Jesus had made during the last days of the earthly portion of His ministry: "Most assuredly, I say to you, he who believes in Me, the works that I do he will do also; and greater works than these he will do, because I go to My Father. And whatever you ask in My name, that I will do, that the Father may be glorified in the Son. If you ask anything in My name, I will do it" (John 14:12-14).

I did not quote that verse in my earlier explanation of the will of God taught and exemplified during Jesus' ministry because it makes little sense until after Pentecost. With the power of the indwelling Lord it becomes one of the most incisive ways to bring together all three of the lights for daily guidance that Meyer suggested. Jesus wants us to do what He did! The works that He did, we are to do. And He has equipped us with His own Spirit to do just that. We are to be lovers, healers, reconcilers, and communicators of joy. He never guides us into anything which will make that impossible.

The power of Pentecost is given us for our relationships with people. The unfolding of the Lord's guidance is to make us gracious, forgiving witnesses. "You shall receive power ... you shall be My witnesses." The two were never separated in the Acts. So much of our quandary about the will of the Lord is that we have tried to pull apart what He galvanized together. The pages of Acts dramatize what can happen when people and their needs become the focus of doing the Lord's will. Loving and caring for people and sharing what Christ means to us and can do for them is the focus of the Lord's will and guidance for our lives. We have been given power to introduce others to Him, to pray with power for the healing of their mind, body, and problems, and to stand with them in intensely empathetical relationships as they struggle to grow.

That may cause a reaction in you: "Wait a moment—I got into this discussion of the Lord's will because I need guidance for my decisions, not to try to help other people with theirs."

But that's just the issue: Helping people is the action step that unlocks knowledge of the will of the Lord. The circumstances about which we are concerned have *people* in them. In fact, the key to solving our circumstances is being the Lord's person to the people in those circumstances. Few of the questions we have about guidance are purely personal, unrelated to others.

Our basic question in discovering guidance is to ask, "Will this decision free me to impact the lives of people with the gospel? Will my primary calling to be a witness be crippled?" We can be sure that any job, marriage, move, investment, or expenditure which leads us away from being a communicator of the Lord is not best for us or His purposes in our lives.

In the Book of Acts we see decisions made around this quality of guidance. Peter and John didn't lead the early church in a symposium of the Lord's will for healing. When they saw the lame man at the gate of the temple, they healed him in Jesus' name. It was the natural thing to do. They were inclined *and* impelled. When they got into trouble with the Sanhedrin for healing and witnessing in Christ's name, they knew that the charge to keep silent was not the Lord's will for them. There were no long discussion groups about civil disobedience. They knew that talking about Christ was their task in the will of the Lord, so they got together to pray for more power to continue.

The room in which they were praying was vividly shaken in affirmation of their determined direction. "And they were all filled with the Holy Spirit, and they spoke the word of God with boldness" (Acts 4:31). The word "filled" is in the aorist passive indicative, showing that a special filling occurred for continuing the task of boldness. In addition to being filled at Pentecost, they were given a replenishment for each new challenge. The image is more of a channel than a reservoir. The followers of Christ were conduits for the flow of power. Each new challenge was given the Spirit's guidance and power to obey.

The qualification for the election of deacons was to find men who were "full of the Holy Spirit and wisdom" (Acts 6:3). And we see that their task was not only serving tables and caring for widows but also sharing the strategy of the expansion of the faith. Stephen was pivotal in a witness that was a prelude to the conversion of Saul of Tarsus, and Philip was sent to Samaria to preach the gospel. And, not by accident, the Lord told Philip to head for Gaza at high noon to be at the right place to meet and introduce to Christ an Ethopian official on his way home from Jerusalem. Stephen didn't know ahead of time that his witness was crucial mainly for what it did to Saul, and Philip had no idea in advance that obeying the Lord's guidance to head for Gaza would result in the conversion of the Ethiopian. They were both ready, willing servants. They witnessed of Christ. His Spirit did the rest.

The conversion of the Apostle Paul was possible because of the action of the Spirit and the willingness of Ananias to go to the persecutor of the church. Ananias didn't have to question the guidance. Telling the Pharisee about Christ was more important than his fear. There was no worked-out plan or theory among the followers of the Way at Damascus to reach Paul for Christ. The Lord got him ready, brought him to the city helpless, and gave Ananias the order to go and announce what the Lord had in mind for him.

The missionary expansion of the church also was clearly under the guidance of the Spirit. He guided each step of the way. The plans unfolded daily. The calling of the Christians to do what Jesus did and to be witnesses was the motive. And getting to more people with the gospel was the method.

When the issue of the Gentile converts arose, the Lord put Peter through an experience on a rooftop in Joppa which radically changed his attitude about extending the gospel to the Gentile world. Here again, he was not preoccupied with developing a strategy of evangelism. The vision the Lord gave him got him ready to be pivotal in initiating a policy which would accept Gentile converts without first having them become full participants in the Hebrew religion. And to confirm the guidance, Peter was called to Caesarea to share the gospel with Gentile Cornelius; here he saw the undeniable blessing of the Spirit on the centurion's whole household.

Later, Paul had great results preaching to the Gentiles. He joined with Peter in convincing the church leaders in Jerusalem that they had better get in line with what the Lord was doing so convincingly. People and their need for Christ, regardless of racial or religious backgrounds, became the basis of the Jerusalem council issuing a statement about Gentile converts. The important thing to note is that it was in response to what the Lord was revealing and the primary concern for people.

The rest of the Book of Acts is a flow of surprises—the Spirit of the Lord intervening with a constant flow of imperatives: Go; speak; do not be afraid.

The reason I have focused on this review of the new humanity in the Book of Acts is to raise the issue of our caution about guidance. Our efforts to be so sure may keep us immobilized with thousands of missed opportunities. We have been promised that we would be given power for our central purpose—people and their need for Christ.

And that brings this whole chapter down to a personal question: Are we part of what Jesus Christ is *continuing* to do? We have met with Him in Galilee on the Mount when He gave us His will for the kingdom. Have we also been to the upper room to receive the power of His Spirit? If we agree that He has a will and we have been endowed with a will, Paul's question is a good one: "Did you receive the Holy Spirit when you believed?"

So much of the contemporary discussion of the baptism of the Holy Spirit misses the mark of our need. The Holy Spirit often is talked about as a special power which is given to a select few. But

He is the baptizer of His people. He is the revealer and the enabler of the will of God. And as such, from within us He guides and gives us power to act on His guidance.

But more must be said. There are not two blessings for a Christian, but two parts of one blessing which frees us to accept a blessed life. And the Spirit is the source of both. He converts us and He fills us. After we begin the Christian life, we are brought to the realization that we cannot live it on our own strength. This realization comes early with some, and sadly, much later with others. But early or late, He baptizes us with power! The essence of the meaning of water baptism gives us the key. It is crucifixion and resurrection. Our control of our will is crucified with Christ, and a new willing will is resurrected. Baptism also means immersion. The baptism of the Spirit is to be immersed into His power. We are covered, clothed, and anointed. We are also filled, and that's the secret. The two blessings of Christ in helping us to know His will are to free us to commit our lives to Him, and then to acknowledge our need to have Him live in us.

You and I know what it is like to be a believer without power, to be a follower of Christ and not be Christ-filled. If you have been brought to the realization of your need for His Spirit, be thankful. If you have never asked Him to live in you, then the power to be guided by Him is available. What happened at Pentecost can and will happen in us. What Christ began, He continued, and continues.

And now, with the help of His indwelling Spirit, we can turn our attention to some sticky questions. Are difficulties the will of God? What's the difference between His perfect and His provisional will? What do we mean when we talk about being "in" or "out" of the Lord's will? What's the difference between the will of God and guidance? All of these questions must be answered in a personal way, rather than with mere philosophic jargon. They all deal with becoming a fully mature person in Christ. And for that we turn to the Apostle Paul. His theology is never divorced from the adventure of becoming a new creature in Christ. What happened to him and what he wrote about it help us to ask the question, "Lord, what do You want me to do?" with the profound, clear thinking of Paul, the greatest Christian thinker who ever lived. He was a man "captured by the will of God." How it happened and what evolved in his life is the compelling focus of the next chapter.

6

Lord, What Do You Want Me to Do?

Saul of Tarsus was filled with disturbing questions as he traveled the long road from Jerusalem to Damascus. It takes six days for a caravan to make the journey—six long days and lonely nights for those questions to tumble about in the brilliant but unsettled mind of the Pharisee. He had been so sure of the cause which had been assigned him by the Sanhedrin. He had pursued it with religious zeal. The challenge perfectly matched his own prejudices about Jesus and His fanatical followers, who claimed that He had risen from the dead. When Saul was put in charge of purging Jerusalem of the followers of the "Way," he pursued his assignment with passion. He persecuted, arrested, and imprisoned as many as he could find in Jerusalem. He learned that there was a large group of Jesus' followers in Damascus. Little did he know, as he traveled there, that a greater will than his own strong will was at work. Strange—here was a man who believed in God and thought he was doing His will, but was actually opposing it.

Saul was a Hebrew and a citizen of the world. He was both a "Hebrew" Jew and a Hellenist—a Greek-speaking Jew. Born and raised the Hebrew son of Hebrew parents in the Hellenistic city of Tarsus, he was later trained under Gamaliel, a great teacher of that time. Saul displayed scholarly excellence and became a leader in the strict branch of the Jewish religion called the Pharisees. Righteousness, the sovereignty of the one true God, obedience to the law and tradition, and religious and moral purity were the central commitments of the Pharisees. The movement had begun to recall Israel to its basic heritage. It attracted those of a legalistic temperament and became a party to dogmatism and exclusivism. And Saul fit both the best and the worst in the Pharisaic religion. Both made him a ready candidate to be the persecutor of the followers of Jesus. He believed Jesus to have been an impostor, an anarchist, and an archenemy of the religion of Israel. The followers of the Galilean Carpenter were even worse—committed, zealous, and impetuous.

But several things had begun to loosen the fabric of Saul's rigid hatred of the followers of Jesus of Nazareth. He had witnessed the courage of those he arrested and carried off to prison. A person with as strong a will as Saul could not overlook the resolute and radiant conviction of these people. Then, he had been astonished when his revered teacher, Gamaliel, had been strongly conciliatory to the church, cautioning the Sanhedrin about too hasty a judgment of the movement. But it was his experience of watching Stephen stoned to death that raised his most persistent questions. He had observed Stephen's courage and fortitude, and most of all his radiant face. The people in the Synagogue of the Freedmen, where Stephen had spoken, were "not able to resist the wisdom and the Spirit by which he spoke" (Acts 6:10). Saul could not forget the look on Stephen's face as he died. Stephen's dying words echoed in Saul's soul: "Look! I see the heavens opened and the Son of Man standing at the right hand of God!" And then this: "Lord Jesus, receive my spirit" (Acts 7:56,59).

And so Saul ruminated. Who are these people—really? What makes them the persons they are? How could someone so obviously brilliant and learned as Stephen talk to a dead Galilean carpenter? Why was Gamaliel cautious about being too harsh on the Way? Most of all, why was Saul himself so impassioned in his persecution and hatred of these people?

Saul of Tarsus was a very troubled man by the time he reached the outskirts of Damascus. There he had an experience which transformed all his questions into one question which he continued asking all of the rest of his life. At high noon, lightning flashed. He and his companions were thrown to the ground. The lightning was followed by "thunder"—a voice from heaven

said, "Saul, Saul, why are you persecuting Me?"
We can only imagine the panic in Saul. "Who are
You, Lord?" (The word for Lord here is
something like "Sir.") The answer came with
undeniable clarity: "I am Jesus, whom you are
persecuting." Saul trembled. Jesus! Alive. It was
true! The voice of the One whom he had said was
not alive and whose followers he had tried to
purge from Israel was there and had spoken to
him. There was no doubt about it.

Astonished and filled with awe, Saul asked
that question which was to become his life question: "Lord, what do You want me to do?"

Jesus' clear command was, "Arise and go into
the city, and you will be told what you must do."
It was Saul's first lesson in the discovery of the
will of the Lord. Getting into the Lord's will and
growing in it as a person is related to following
the first orders we receive even if they don't
make sense immediately. The Lord could have ef-
fected Saul's conversion right there, but He
wanted to use His people in Damascus for that.
Saul's arrogance and pride had to be broken. His
will had to be ready.

When he arose from the ground, he was blind.
The imperious Saul had to be led into the city by
his own men. The transformation of a human being was in process. In Damascus he had to wait
again, sitting helplessly blind. But the Lord had a
plan for the transformation of Saul from
darkness and the church from fear. Both were
blessed by the way He did it. Ananias, who had
been on Saul's "hit list," was appointed to go as a

communicator of the Lord's grace and to announce to him the Lord's amazing plan and purpose for his life. We can imagine what Ananias went through. Saul of Tarsus? Our feared persecutor? He was told to tell this same Saul that the Lord had appointed him to be His chosen vessel to bear the Lord's name "before Gentiles, kings, and the children of Israel."

What Ananias said to Saul when he reached him is very significant in the revelation of the will of the Lord to Saul afterward: "Brother Saul, the Lord Jesus, who appeared to you on the road as you came, has sent me that you may receive your sight and be filled with the Holy Spirit." The living Spirit of God now entered the ready and willing Saul. The scales fell from his eyes, and he began to see with both his eyes and his mind. His baptism was an outward sign to him and the church that he had been baptized inwardly with the Spirit of Christ.

That infilling of the Spirit was crucial for the transformation of Saul's thinking about who Christ was and for what Saul himself was to become as a man in Christ. What he later wrote to the Corinthians is an apt description of his own condition in those early days after his conversion and baptism by the Spirit: "For if there is first a willing mind, it is accepted according to what one has, and not according to what he does not have" (2 Corinthians 8:12). So Saul began using his now-willing mind. He was accepted by the church, began his first preaching, and experienced the wondrous joy of his new relationship with Christ.

Now the main point. In Galatians 2:1 Paul says that it was 14 years between his conversion and baptism in Christ's Spirit and his first missionary journey. That's a long time before getting into active service on the front line! He was sent to Tarsus for his preparation for a ministry which was to change the course of history. About 10 of those 14 years were spent there. We wonder if he felt "shelved" or forgotten. What he said and did when he began his ministry convinces us of the contrary. In those years he was on the Potter's wheel, being molded into a new person in every fiber of his thought, will and character. In communication with Christ Himself, the tissues of Paul's brain were reformed around his new conviction: Jesus Christ is Lord. Emerson said, "A man is what he thinks about all day long." Paul became what he thought and prayed about for 14 years!

What the apostle preached and wrote came out of the distilled clarity of that preparation. And the thought and prayer fashioned an obedient and energetic will. That's the reason doing the will of the Lord became the only passion of his life. Union with Christ was the firm foundation on which he built the structure of all his thought. What he wrote the Galatians puts it clearly: "I have been crucified with Christ; it is no longer I who live, but Christ lives in me; and the life which I now live in the flesh I live by faith in the Son of God, who loved me and gave Himself for me" (Galatians 2:20). The only thing that mattered was his new creation in Christ (Galatians 6:15).

The same note was sounded to the Corinthians: "Therefore, if anyone is in Christ, he is a new creation; old things have passed away; behold, all things have become new" (2 Corinthians 5:17). Jesus Christ and life in Him were the focus of the will of God for Paul.

He began his epistles with bold assurance: "Paul, called to be an apostle of Jesus Christ through the will of God . . . ." There was no arrogance in that; he had been captured by the will of God in Christ Jesus. His experience and subsequent metamorphosis had changed him from a persecutor to a propagator of the gospel. The Lord had been the Author of it all. Just as clearly as Paul could say, "God was in Christ reconciling the world" (2 Corinthians 5:19)—the will of God surging, active, creative, personal—so too he could say that this same powerful force had integrated and energized his will to accept the awesome calling to be numbered among the apostles.

This exemplifies all that we've said so far about how the will works. The mind of Christ impacted the mind of Paul; his mind was reoriented around Christ. His will, which had previously been in the bondage of willfulness, was marshaled to desire the Lord and all that He had planned for him. His mind signaled new orders to his brain. Paul's Lord was marching on! And the called and appointed apostle fell in behind, following in His cadences and commands. There is no finer "before-and-after" account of the transformation of a person's will in Christian history.

The result was that Paul's practical, working faith contained three dynamics. First, his purpose was to do the Lord's will. Second, the Lord had taken on Himself the responsibility of special care for Paul, and would make clear the specifics of His plan for daily obedience. And third, Paul therefore had no need to fear anything or consider any assignment impossible. Those three things are evidenced in everything Paul said about the will of the Lord and dared to attempt because of it—because of Him!

Now let's look at some specific passages and see how this was worked out in the busy life of an active and tireless missionary sent to change the course of history.

In the first chapter of Ephesians Paul speaks of the pleasure, mystery, and counsel of God's will. He wanted the new converts in Christ to build their discipleship on the same convictions which had become so clear to him in his own life.

Our assurance is that God has "predestined us to adoption as sons by Jesus Christ to Himself, according to the good pleasure of His will" (Ephesians 1:5). The adoption proceedings were finished on Calvary. When Christ died for us, the transfer was sealed. God had you and me in mind when He reconciled the world. It was His pleasure, desire, and delight to include us in His plan. This focuses the will of God not as a foreboding frown on history but as the pleasure of God. His love could not leave us out: He was and is pleased to call us His sons and daughters. What He said at Christ's baptism He says of us: "This is My beloved Son, in whom I am well pleased" (Matthew 3:17).

The same stirring theme of pleasure in God's heart is reintroduced with further harmony as Paul continues his symphony of words to explain the will of God in Ephesians 1:9: "Having made known to us the mystery of His will, according to His good pleasure which He purposed in Himself." The veil of mystery about God's will has been lifted; He has been both Stage Manager and Primary Actor in the drama. He both opened the curtain and appeared on the stage of history to show us that His will is "purposed in Himself." He is His will! He comes to us in Christ, the full impact of His plan and purpose. That is made clear in the next verse: "That in the dispensation of the fullness of the times he might gather together in one all things in Christ, both which are in heaven and which are on earth—in Him" (Ephesians 1:10). But press on!

This pleasure of God is expressed in the counsel of His will. It means his pleasure had a purpose: "We have obtained an inheritance, being predestined according to the purpose of Him who works all things according to the counsel of His will, that we who first trusted in Christ should be to the praise of His glory" (Ephesians 1:11,12).

You will remember that two Greek words are used for the will of God: thelēma and boulēma. Thelēma means God's desire, and boulēma His

immutable plan. The first calls for our cooperation; the second is done regardless. In Acts 2:23
Christ's death and resurrection are part of the
boulēma of God: the atonement could not be stopped. It looked like the crucifixion was the will of
evil men; it was that, but behind the events
leading up to the cross was the irrevocable will of
God in preparation for the resurrection, the
glorification of Christ, and His return to
transform the wills of those called to be His
disciples in order to make them into new
creatures as a part of the new creation.

In this passage from Ephesians 1:11 the word
thelēma is used. The counsel, or purpose, of
God's *thelēma* requires our response. But there
is more than an offer and an anxious wait for our
response. God's will is higher than ours and can
instigate our response and cooperation.

This is asserted in Romans 9. Here Paul talks
about the will of God with the stronger word
boulēma, implying His impelling intention for you
and me. "For who has resisted His will?" (verse
19), the apostle asks. He goes on to use the image
of the potter and the clay. The point for you and
me is that God has elected us to know His will and
has the power to shape us into vessels to live for
His glory with willingness.

Can we resist? Yes and no. It is my personal
belief that when God singles us out, He will bring
us around—gently, mercifully. He works in us to
free us to claim our inheritance. Could Paul have
closed the door on Ananias and spent the rest of
His life in a blind stupor? One side of our ex-

perience makes it seem so. But we sense God's *boulēma* will at work in that dramatic conscription to new life in Christ. The same power that raised Jesus from the dead was working. God did not obliterate Paul's will; He crucified it and resurrected it. The immutable currents of God's purpose were surging down the riverbed of His plan. Paul didn't so much step into it; he was caught up in it and carried on to what the Lord had prepared. That's the mystery of His will.

The same essential truth is necessary to understand the difference between God's perfect and His provisional will. Paul deals with the sublime capacity that God has given us to know His perfect will. Romans 12:1,2 tells us how we can know it: "I beseech you therefore, brethren, by the mercies of God, that you present your bodies a living sacrifice, holy, acceptable to God, which is your reasonable service. And do not be conformed to this world, but be transformed by the renewing of your mind, that you may prove what is that good and acceptable and perfect will of God."

For clarity, let's think about God's perfect will as meaning that we know, love, and glorify Him in all that we say and do in life's circumstances. Each situation in our daily lives holds the possibility of what God intends, or, if we resist for a time, what He will do to work that into the fabric of His ultimate will for us. He will not be outmaneuvered by us! Even our mistakes and failures will be used to help us grow in His grace. A wrong choice at some fork in the road of our lives may lead us on to a place that He did not intend, but He will make that place a waystation in the travel plans of life He has for us. He doesn't call us back to the fork in the road, but He makes us unsatisfied with what we thought was our destination. He opens up another route to get us onto the main road we missed at the crossroads.

But you and I have agreed that we want clearer guidance at those crossroads. There are three things that we can do. A careful study of the admonitions Paul gives in this Romans 12:1,2 passage provides us with some very valuable steps we can take after we accept that God's will is Jesus Christ, life in Him, His life in us, and becoming a new creature in Him. The very fact that Paul opens this statement with a reference to the mercies of God that he has talked about in the first 11 chapters of Romans is very significant. These mercies all focus in Christ and become the motive of following the imperatives for guidance that Paul suggests so strongly.

First, we are to "present our bodies a living sacrifice." It is helpful to think of "bodies" as more than either the body apart from the brain or the brain apart from the mind. I think Paul is talking about our lives—our self-consciousness, soul, mind, brain, nervous system, physical anatomy, and all that makes us a distinct, separate human being. All this is unified in the thoughts, desires, and decisions which motivate the behavior of our lives. If we agree that in a spiritual sense the will is the whole person active, then Paul's admonition implies "present your wills"—the whole of you and the self-determining portion which controls what you do and become. A helpful cross-reference is 1 Corinthians 6:19,20: "Do you not know that your body is the temple of the Holy Spirit who is in you, whom you have from God, and you are not your own? For you were bought with a price; therefore glorify God in your body and in your spirit, which are God's." The "body" thus means the whole of us—a gift of God. This is what we are to offer as a living sacrifice.

It means complete dedication. In the sacrifices of the temple, a living animal was the only acceptable offering. But our minds dart back to David's prayer of confession in Psalm 51 and his realization that God does not delight in burnt offerings. "The sacrifices of God are a broken spirit, a broken and a contrite heart" (Psalm 51:17). We must give that which is "holy," which means belonging to God and set apart by Him for Himself. Our lives as saints (the word has its root in "holy") are to be offered without reservation. That alone is "acceptable to God." Anything less will not open us to His will and guidance.

This is our reasonable service. The meaning is "rational." What we do as an act of will is the fruition of thought and decision. Offering our wills to God is the ultimate expression of Christian service. Without that, any service we do is inadequate and often misguided, or it can become a substitute for God Himself. How often Christians have done some service as an evasion of doing God's will!

The next admonition is that we are not to

become "conformed to this world." Paul literally means "Stop being shaped by this world." The Greek word "world," or age, is aiōn, and is used in the biblical sense of a social order that takes no note of God or His will. Archbishop Trench used to interpret that as "all the floating mass of thoughts, opinions, maxims, speculations, hopes, impulses, aims, aspirations" which are part of the world around us. When we know that the essential will of God for us is Christ and life in Him and He in us, we no longer look to non-Christians or cultural values for the signs of His guidance. Again Paul's life question is the difference: "Lord, what do You want me to do?" Paul would never have become the great man "in Christ" he became if he had relied on either the religious value system of his fellow Jews or the secular world of the culture of the Greco-Roman world in which he moved.

Instead, we are to be "transformed by the renewing of your mind." This is the third admonition. The Greek verb for transformed, metamor-phōo, is the root of our English word "metamorphosis." The essence of the meaning is the changing of outward appearances to agree with the inner self. The word for repentance, metanoia, is the way this happens. Our outward appearance and conduct are to be congruent with our inner nature. The way Paul found that this happens is by the "renewing of the mind." W.E. Vine said that the mind in this context is the faculty of knowing, "the seat of reflective consciousness, comprising the faculties of perception and understanding, and those of feeling, judging, and determining."*

Paul saw the source of this renewal of our mind in receiving the mind of Christ, who is both the Example and the Motivator of life. The more our minds are conditioned by Him, the more like Him we become. "Let this mind be in you which was also in Christ Jesus" (Philippians 2:5) explains this, as does "We have the mind of Christ" (1 Corinthians 2:16). Daily guidance is the transformation of our behavior, actions, and activities to be in keeping with a Christ-transformed mind.

There are three ways that we "prove" the perfect will of God for us. "Prove" means to know surely with a trustworthy knowledge. The term is also used for purifying metals or testing their strength. All of the three admonitions for guidance in the will of God that Paul gave us are part of that refining and testing process. They are the precious keys for the triple-locked secret of guidance—commitment of our will, freedom from dependence on contemporary, cultural values which are not rooted in Christ, and bringing our outward life into conformity with the indwelling Christ through moment-by-moment renewal of our relationship with Him. Use those keys, and God's perfect will becomes clear. Actually, the circle is repeated endlessly: We ask for guidance; we test what comes to mind by the

---

*W.E. Vine, *Expository Dictionary of New Testament Words* (Oliphants Ltd., 1981), p. 69.

mind of Christ; we act to the best of our understanding. Knowing and doing are inseparable. To know is to do, and to do is to know more. Lord, what do You want me to do?

And when we miss or resist the answer? The Lord's provisional will is done, which (if we are willing) will be worked into His perfect will, that which accomplishes His purpose to do His work now and get us to heaven. When we are "in" Christ, we are not "out" of His will. We may frustrate His best for us, but the worst that happens to us can be used to accomplish His best.

How about other people and circumstances around us that bring frustration and difficulty into our lives? Are they part of the Lord's will? What about tragedies, sickness, and discouragements which we did not cause? The danger is that anything we can't quite explain or understand gets dumped in the catchall, "It must be the will of God." I hear people say this when loved ones die or the bottom falls out of life. We also blame a lot of germs, human malice, and social evil on the will of God. What kind of God does that make Him? There's a great difference in what He *wills* and what He *permits*. He created this a free world; He made us persons and not puppets, and He allowed the self-imposed bondage of our wills in self-centeredness. Our free world is also a fallen world; it is not what God intended for us. But because love involves choice, He gives us freedom. What humankind has done to life and our environment is not what God had in mind.

But God's perfect will can be done in spite of

the negative things which happen. As we trust Him with them, using the three keys we talked about above, He makes them part of His provisional will to move us on in accomplishing His perfect will.

The apostle is very honest with us about his own personal struggles to live in the Lord's will. It is comforting to read the last portion of Romans 7 and the opening of Romans 8, because they describe both his battle and his victory. Read this if you have the apostle on an idealic pedestal or thought it was all easy after his conversion. "For the good that I will to do, I do not do; but the evil I will not to do, that I practice. Now if I do what I will not to do, it is no longer I who do it, but sin that dwells in me. I find then a law, that evil is present with me, the one who wills to do good. For I delight in the law of God according to the inward man. But I see another law in my members, warring against the law of my mind, and bringing me into captivity to the law of sin which is in my members. O wretched man that I am!" (Romans 7:19-24).

Some say that Paul was describing his experience before the Damascus road conversion, and others that he was just empathizing with the Christians at Rome over their struggles. What would you say? Have you ever had a struggle like that after becoming a Christian? I suspect we all have. We belong to Christ, and yet, for a time, we fall back into willing what is less than the Lord's best, sometimes in rebellious opposition. We are in serious trouble only if we don't see this and confess it. Self-justification or defensiveness over the kind of struggle that Paul describes would be a sign of deep spiritual sickness. We are in danger when we call evil good. The fact that Paul didn't have to pretend to have it all together must have built really strong bridges of communication with his readers. It does that for us as we read it today. There are times when we don't "feel" like even asking what the Lord's guidance is. We get into a willful mood of trying to run things ourselves. Then, when we see the mess this causes for us and the loved ones around us, we cry out for help.

Read on in what Paul said. He recognized that he was a wretched man, and when he asked who could help him want the Lord's will as his own will, he was brought to this affirmation: "I thank God—through Christ Jesus our Lord! So then, with the mind I myself serve the law of God, but with the flesh the law of sin. There is therefore now no condemnation to those who are in Christ Jesus, who do not walk according to the flesh, but according to the Spirit. For the law of the Spirit of life in Christ Jesus has made me free from the law of sin and death. For what the law could not do in that it was weak through the flesh, God did by sending His own Son in the likeness of sinful flesh, on account of sin: He condemned sin in the flesh, that the righteous requirement of the law might be fulfilled in us who do not walk according to the flesh but according to the Spirit. For those who live according to the flesh set their minds on the things of the flesh, but those who live accord-

ing to the Spirit, the things of the Spirit"
(Romans 7:25—8:5).

Paul made it through the struggle and knew
that the secret was living according to the
Spirit's indwelling power. Real growth in the
Christian life is accomplished when we have an
early-warning signal of those times of resistance
and cry out for the Spirit to refocus our mind so
that our will once again becomes the servant of
guided thought and not the master of our mind.

Paul also went through a great deal of suffering. In each dilemma or difficulty, he asked in
substance, "Lord, what do You want out of
this?" rather than "Lord, why did You get me
into this?" That freed Paul to say, "For I consider
that the sufferings of this present time are not
worthy to be compared with the glory which shall
be revealed in us . . . . Yet in all these things we
are more than conquerors through Him who
loved us. For I am persuaded that neither death
nor life, nor angels nor principalities nor powers,
nor things present nor things to come, nor height
nor depth, nor any other created thing, shall be
able to separate us from the love of God which is
in Christ Jesus our Lord" (Romans 8:18,37-39).

That's the kind of courage and conviction that
comes when we ask, "Lord, what do You want me
to do?"

Paul's triumphant faith was that the Lord was
at work within him, making His specific will
known each day along the way. He shared that
conviction with the church at Philippi: "For it is
God who works in you both to will and to do for

His good pleasure'' (Philippians 2:13). That's the secret of life in the will of God. The word for work in Greek is from *energeō*. The omnipotent power of God is the source of the energizing force in you and me to want His will and to respond. The thanksgiving goes to Him. We can relax and let it happen. He is at work in us doing it! No wonder Paul could write the Romans about his guided plan to be with them. The same clarity that had been expressed to the Philippians is obvious again: "that I may come to you with joy by the will of God, and may be refreshed together with you'' (Romans 15:32).

I received a letter recently from a friend with whom I had experienced that joy and refreshment. We had met at a conference where I spoke on the will of the Lord. I had focused on becoming a new creature in Christ as the purpose of His will. As is often my custom, I ended my last message with "Why not?"

Why not live life in Christ without reservation? Why not allow Him to transform our will? Why not accept the character transplant He wants to perform so that we can think, will, and act as His liberated persons? Why not indeed?

My new friend decided to ask himself "Why not?" and dared to answer. It led him to Paul's question, "Lord, what do You want me to do?" and to the commitment to do some things he had been putting off in his discipleship, as well as to some new things the Lord had been putting on his agenda. He wrote me to communicate his gratitude. He used a way that he knew I would appreciate. He knows of my love for Scotland and chose to relate an account from his life to express his new joy in the will of the Lord.

An old Scots woman by the name of Mrs. Ferguson used to greet him in the mornings with the expression, "Ah, Jim, is it yourself that's out this morning?" The man related that the woman now has gone on to the next phase of her eternal life in heaven. "But if she were here now to ask me that question again," he wrote, "I would say to her in sure confidence, 'Ah, Mrs. Ferguson, it's myself that's out this morning. Indeed it is!' "

And the man who's out is an integrated person around the will of God—a newly transformed man because of the renewing of his mind.

So often it's less than ourselves that's out any morning, or any time of the day or night. When the Lord makes our will His own and comes to live in us with energizing power, there's a real self, an authentic person, to be out front in honest, authentic, unstudied joy. Our wills are no longer bent in on ourselves but are now focused on the Lord and on others.

Robert Mounce, the President of Whitworth College, ended a statement about the purpose of higher Christian education which applies to our whole life in the Lord's will: "So that later in life, when you knock on yourself, someone answers." What I've tried to say in this part of our conversation is that consistently asking, "Lord, what do You want me to do?" develops a character in Christ ready to answer not only when we knock, but when others knock as well.

7

A Future Without Fear

We're all concerned about the future. We want to know what the future holds. We'd like a clear prospectus of what's ahead. We wish God wouldn't give us the specifics a day or a year at a time, but the whole picture. Right now, Lord!

But if we had that, we could go off and do it without Him. He gives us enough knowledge of His will to live one day at a time. That's not easy to handle when our worries over the future invade the present. And so we become anxious about tomorrow and miss today.

My conversations with Christians indicate that there's a big yawning gap between what we say about trusting in God's will, and the fretful lives we live. Many are afraid of living adventuresomely and are troubled about dying courageously. Therefore, each perplexity is a little death.

The fear of the future is heightened with sickness or the death of a loved one. We look in the mirror and are reminded that we are not getting younger, or handling the signs of our own human limitations very well. If God would only tell us what the future for us is going to be like!

We don't talk about these feelings very much. Our fear of the future is an emotionally supercharged subject. We'll happily talk about the theology of the will of God, but sharing our panic about the future is a taboo subject. How can we really trust the future to the will of God?

The basis for future-hope is the resurrection. Christ's resurrection not only defeated the power of death and evil, but it is the formula for freedom from the death-grip that uncertainty about the future has on our souls. The subject that we talked about earlier is in need of a more thorough treatment. The same power that raised Jesus from the dead is available to you and me, not only at the time of our physical death, but also in our concern over how things will work out in the future. The assurance that we are offered is that the Lord can and will intervene to pull us out of the doldrums of dread and discouragement. He raises the dead, but He also resurrects our deepest concerns. He steps in with power to do what we could not have imagined or dared to anticipate. After one of those times, we look back and say, "Why was I so worried?" But the joy seeps away in the next challenge.

I'm convinced that we need a resurrection faith to trust God's will for the future.

Recently I went through the experience of the death of my mother. I was privileged to be with her as she went through the long, hard days and nights before her life was resurrected out of her tired, paralyzed body. Physically, it was not an easy death. There were three people involved in my last conversation with her before she slipped into a coma. My mother and I—and the Lord. We prayed together. When we finished, she thanked me for my part in the conversation with the Lord. My reply was, "Mother, you taught me how to pray." She smiled and said, "Praise the Lord!"

That dear lady lived and died with the assurance of the resurrection. Many years of her life were invaded by financial needs, concern over my father's health, and the challenge of raising a family through the later years of the Depression. But her deep, personal relationship with Christ, whom she loved with all her heart, gave her hope in each perplexity. She expected the Lord's intervention in her needs and was not disappointed. Trust in the Lord's will meant that He would provide.

Long before I acknowledged His election of my life, she had claimed it and thanked God in advance that in His timing I would become a Christian. She had pictured in her mind my conversion and call and kept praying with gratitude that it would happen. She faced my younger sister's and my dad's death with the same trust. Her own death was experienced with no fear of the future.

Death for you was not a hopeless end;
You simply rose to meet your Loyal Friend!

Trust in the Lord's will for our future is the result of resurrection living by resurrection power.

My most exciting Easter happened to me one August. The experience has made every day Easter for me. It was then that I realized that the resurrection spells the final defeat of the fear of the future.

It happened one afternoon when I was in Jerusalem. I had gone to a lonely place outside the Old City called Gordon's Garden Tomb. It is believed by many to be the authentic site of Christ's crucifixion and resurrection. My travels in Israel had brought me to the most significant places of the radical interventions of God in biblical history. I had kept this final site for the last, savoring in my mind the possibility of a personal Easter in August. When I entered the garden, I climbed a long walkway to a place that looks up on a hillside. The cragged granite displays to this day an outline of the skull. Golgotha!

There I stood for what must have been an hour of refocusing in my mind's eye the excruciating suffering and pain of the cross. Then in my heart I heard the loving impact of His voice: "I did it for you, Lloyd. You are forgiven through the blood I shed here." As I walked back down into the garden below, my heart sang with gratitude—I am loved, accepted, forgiven, reconciled.

Familiar hymns came floating through the ready tissues of an open mind: "Beneath the cross of Jesus I fain would take my stand," and "There's power, power, wonder-working power in the blood, in the blood of the Lamb," and "When I survey the wondrous cross." The recommitment to a central task was articulated in my soul. I said with Paul, "For I am determined not to know anything among you except Jesus Christ and Him crucified" (1 Corinthians 2:2). No one ever sees that the tomb is empty except from the scaffolding of the cross.

In the garden I walked into the open tomb. I had done that before during visits to Jerusalem, but somehow this was different. The Presence I felt on Golgotha remained with me stronger than ever. I sat down in front of the open tomb determined not to leave until I had a fresh realization of the resurrection. It happened in a way I did not expect. Suddenly a chill ran up my spine. A negative suggestion captured my thoughts. What if the resurrection hadn't happened? What then? For a long time I allowed my thoughts to ruminate on the ghastly possibility. Chewing over each bitter bite into the dreadful possibility, I pictured what 2000 years of history might have been like: Christ discredited, a Savior dead in His grave for pilgrims to visit as they do David's tomb, no church to reach the world with evangelical urgency, no hope to preach with zeal, no victory over death. My heart ached with the disillusioning thought. My sins would not be forgiven; my insecurity would remain unhealed; my vision for life would have to be crammed into the brief years of this life. Alarm. Panic. Discouragement. In a brief span of thought, I was in touch with the millions on earth who are without Christ and without hope.

The Lord put me through it. His gentle voice sounded in my soul again: "Now you know the plight of the world. I have allowed you to think and feel this through so that what I did here so long ago might make you more than a preacher of the resurrection, but an Easter person. The same power that raised Jesus from the dead will be yours every day of your life." And in response I said out loud, "Hallelujah! Christ is risen. He is risen indeed!"

The experience of living with the vision of a world without the resurrection brought to mind the words Paul wrote to the Corinthians in history's first complete description in writing of the power of the resurrection. The Corinthian Christians had been troubled by both Hebrew theologians and Greek philosophers who had tried to undermine their belief that Christ rose from the dead. Paul received word of this frightening drift into doubt of his beloved Corinthian converts. In response, he empathetically entered into their equivocation. He crawled into their skins and lived in their troubled minds.

In profound love he wrote words that stabbed them awake to the danger of their delusion: "Now if Christ is preached that He has been raised from the dead, how do some among you say that there is no resurrection of the dead? But if there is no resurrection from the dead, then Christ is not risen. And if Christ is not risen, then our preaching is vain and your faith is also vain. Yes, and we are found false witnesses of God, because we have testified of God that He raised up Christ, whom He did not raise up—if in fact the dead do not rise. For if the dead do not rise, then Christ is not risen. And if Christ is not risen, your faith is futile; you are still in your sins! Then also those who have fallen asleep in Christ have perished. If in this life only we have hope in Christ, we are of all men the most pitiable" (1 Corinthians 15:12-19).

Incisively Paul forced the Corinthians to live through what life would be like without the resurrection. In substance he was saying, "All right, dear sisters and brothers, if you meddle with the resurrection, know what you are doing —you are denying God, disbelieving the gospel, debilitating your faith, disowning your redemption, declaring death an ending, and demanding that the abundant life be crammed into the brief years of an earthly existence." Shocking? Yes!

But I am strangely thankful that the Corinthians went through their time of doubt, because their negativism has brought forth a carefully reasoned, positive statement of the resurrection. I want to deal with each part of it to heighten our own realization of the power of the resurrection as the confidence in the will of the Lord for our future. Paul offers us a sixfold progression of thought and experience of the meaning and present power of the resurrection. Allow me to reorder the unfolding drama of Paul's mind.

First, the resurrection was God's final defeat of impossibilities. We deny God, not just Christ, when we question the resurrection. The salient verse which focuses our thinking at the head-waters is "God was in Christ, reconciling the world to Himself." That says it all! Put that triumphant fact with this verse from Romans 4:24,25: "[We] believe in Him who raised up Jesus our Lord from the dead, who was delivered up for our offenses, and was raised because of our justification." Christ's death and resurrection can never be separated. They are one act of the one and only God. The issue was the right-eousness of God. As such, He had to do something about our sin. He could not overlook it or condone it. An atonement had to be made. A sacrifice, an eternal benchmark of restitution. As we have said, the cross was what we deserved, and Christ took it for us as the Mediator between a just God and a sinful humanity. Forgiveness was imputed on the cross, but justification, rightness with God, was inculcated with the resurrection. It was God's vindication of the cross, His seal of af-firmation of the finished work of salvation. When Christ died, our sins died; when He arose, we were resurrected into a sublime status of the redeemed.

Deny the resurrection, and you have a God of forgiveness, but not of power. And what dif-ference does it make if we are forgiven by the death of One who has never defeated the grave?

That leads to the second of Paul's guantlet

challenges to those who trifle with the resurrection: "Our preaching is vain." The word "vain" means *empty*. The central theme of the preaching of the early church was the resurrection. As John Knox said in his book *Jesus, Lord and Christ*, "The primitive Christian community was not a memorial society with its eyes fastened on a departed master; it was a dynamic community created around a living and present Lord." Peter's first sermon after Pentecost displays this commitment to the center of the center: "Him, being delivered by the determined counsel and foreknowledge of God, you have taken by lawless hands, have crucified, and put to death; whom God raised up, having loosed the pains of death, because it was not possible that He should be held by it" (Acts 2:23,24). The reason Peter and John were arrested was because they boldly identified the resurrected Christ as the only source of their power to heal a lame man. "As they spoke to the people, the priests, the captain of the temple, and the Sadducees came upon them, being greatly disturbed that they taught the people and preached in Jesus the resurrection from the dead." The cross revealed the nature of God; the resurrection exposed His power.

How empty the apostolic preaching would have been without the resurrection! The fact of a loving Savior dying out of love for sinful people would not have sent the disciples out into the then-known world with an impelling, life-changing message. Rather, it was the living, indwelling Christ who motivated them. He was their Companion and Trailblazer, infusing them with power. If death had ended Him, there would have been no gospel to preach.

For us, if we have no gospel of the resurrection, we are left with an endless succession of impossibilities: Christ is left in the grave, a lovely memory, a heroic figure. But the resurrection tells us that nothing is impossible for Him! Now we have a living hope.

The resurrection is absolutely necessary in order for us to take Christ seriously. His message was punctuated by repeated promises that He would rise from the dead. In fact, He told His disciples exactly what would happen: "Behold, we are going up to Jerusalem, and the Son of Man will be betrayed to the chief priests and to the scribes; and they will condemn Him to death, and deliver Him to the Gentiles to mock and to scourge and to crucify. And the third day He will rise again" (Matthew 20:18,19). Then there was this bold statement about Himself: "Destroy this temple, and in three days I will raise it up." And His statement about the sign of Jonah that He would be three days and three nights in the heart of the earth and then rise from the dead. If there were no resurrection, what about Christ's confident assurance that He had the power to lay down His life and raise it up again? What about those tender promises given in the Upper Room just before He was crucified? What shall we do with His pledge to return and to be with us? If some of Jesus' sayings were false wish-dreams, what shall we do with the rest? All are discredited if even one is an exaggeration. Who needs one more teacher, or the greatest philosopher who ever lived, or the most sublime example of humanity, if what He taught and the truths about life He revealed and the model of life He exposed are all negated by a crucifixion that ended Him.

Auguste Comte once told Thomas Carlyle that he was going to start a new religion to replace Christianity. "Very good," replied Carlyle. "All you will have to do is to be crucified, rise again on the third day, and get the world to believe you are still alive. Then your new religion will have a chance." And that's exactly why Christ can speak to us. If He had not been raised, the meaning of what He said would not have lasted a generation.

If Christ did not rise, we have no gospel. Instead, we have suggestions but no solution, analysis of life but no atonement, wringing our hands over impossibilities but no ringing message for our impossibilities. If Christ did not win, we are defeated!

Now press on with Paul. If Christ has not been raised, not only is God impotent and our message ineffective, but our faith is futile. We have trusted our destiny to a Savior who can do nothing for us. Faith is God's gift. It is born in the soul of one who hears the good news of the death and resurrection of Christ. There is no faith without that living assurance. Faith is not a human capacity developed out of strength of character; it is inseparably related to Golgotha and an empty tomb. Without that as a beginning, there is no faith for daily living in impossibilities. But when faith is born out of Good Friday and Easter, it grows to encompass all of life's challenges and responsibilities. We can trust all our needs to the Savior risen from the dead. Take that victory away, and all we are left with is yearning, wishful thinking, empty hopes, and strenuous struggles to make things work out. What would life be without faith?

Because Christ lives, the four most impossible things in life can happen:

1. People can be changed.
2. Events can be altered.
3. Relationships can be healed.
4. Love can win over hatred.

But Paul goes on. If Christ has not been raised, we are still in our sins. Recapture those times of confession when you asked for forgiveness and thought you were set free. Reflect on all that you thought was washed away. Consider what it would be like to live again with all those incriminating mistakes and failures. Take them all back if Christ is not risen! No dead savior can blot out the record. No Galilean carpenter can communicate that you are loved in spite of the mess you and I have made. And if we have not been forgiven, our power to forgive must also be relinquished. Who but the forgiven can accept the inadequacies and injustices of others? Take back all the hurt done to you, the cutting words, the dehumanizing judgments! Where are you

now, if Christ has not been raised?
>*And how do I know He's the living God?*
>*In corruption of sin I lay dead,*
>*But life everlasting came into me when*
>*"Thy sins are forgiven," He said.*

Only a vindicated, risen Lord has the authority to forgive us today. John Wesley was right: "It takes as great a miracle to bring a man or woman from the sepulchre of sin as to bring Christ's body from the tomb." And yet, you and I are living testimony that it can happen. We are the resurrection miracles today!

And there's more. If Christ has not been raised, all of our loved ones and friends who have died did not make it through the valley of the shadow of death to an eternal joy. Their death was an ending. Stand again with beloved people and watch them die knowing that death has the final word. Huddle aimlessly about the grave and watch the coffin lowered, knowing that all your cherished person was is now lying in the grave . . . body and spirit. If death has the last word, if this final body is all there is to life, then grief and sorrow will not only punctuate, but will pervade, our days. There is no hope of seeing loved ones again. We must endure their death as a bitter end. Life is frail, and death is final! We have no hope with which to answer Job's question, "If a man die, shall he live again?" Nothing but a nauseating "No!" which makes our hearts groan and wretch. We are left with heavenly-scented funeral parlors, hopeless eulogies of a person's goodness with no reference to God's greatness, and graves marked by stones on which are recorded the length, but not the liberation, of life. All that—if Christ is not risen!

A crucial part of the assurance that our loved ones who died in Christ are alive with Him is that they are mysteriously a part of our life as the "great cloud of witnesses." I think of them as angels pulling for us, helping us to do our best, standing with us in times of trial.

We are not alone. Christ is with us and so are all our loved ones who have become part of our cheering section. And what would they tell us if we could hear? "Be sure of your eternal life! The life on earth is only a beginning, an inch on the yardstick of eternity."

All of life must be crammed into the brief years of this life if we let go of the resurrection. That's Paul's final *reductio ad absurdum.* "If in this life only we have hope in Christ, we are of all men the most pitiable." Indeed! If we believe that this life is all there is, we will live it shabbily when we try to pack this life full because we believe that all we have is a frustrating trek to the grave. We will die "inch by inch and play at little games." People who live in the perspective of an eternal life experience the abundant life here and now. A Christian is a person for whom heaven has begun; death is only a transition. There's a trite saying, "To live with the saints in heaven, that will be glory; to live with people on earth, that's a different story!" Not true. When we know we are alive forever, we live with people in a very different way. Our gratitude for our eternal life is expressed in our daily life. The focus of our will is no longer what we want but what people around us need.

The amazing truth is that people who have believed in Christ's resurrection and have claimed their own resurrection live with a disentangled freedom. Nothing has ultimate claim on them except the Lord's will. The only Person to please is the risen Lord. Things are secondary. Problems are but a prelude to new evidences of radical intervention from the resurrected Lord of new beginnings. "If the Son has set you free, you are free indeed!" He promised. He raises us out of the tombs of frustration and fear. As Paul Tournier put it, "Life is not a static state but a succession of new births." Everything matters creatively because nothing matters ultimately except our relationship with Him. When we experience the reality of the resurrection, we come alive now and live forever.

This life is in preparation for eternity. We are not finished when we die physically; we go on growing. Think of the most cherished gifts of this life—love, joy, peace, hope. Multiply these a billion times, and you have only begun to explain the blessedness of heaven. As Victor Hugo put it at age 70, "Winter is on my head, but Spring is in my heart. I have not said one thousandth part of what is in me."

That's the big "but" which buttresses Paul's conviction as he moves from logical disputation with the floundering Corinthians to liberating declaration. *But!* "But now Christ is risen from the dead, and has become the firstfruits of those who have fallen asleep." An understanding of the terms "firstfruits" and "fallen asleep" heightens our appreciation of the triumphant hope of the resurrection in the Lord's will for our future.

The firstfruits were the first stalks of grain brought to the temple and waved before the altar as foreview and promise of the Lord's bountiful harvest. Christ's resurrection is the assurance of our resurrection from a living death to a deathless life. "Those who have fallen asleep" is a phrase Paul uses throughout his epistles to mean death. The dead who have died in full belief in Christ's blood and resurrection are also raised as He was raised. But that's not all! You and I are also the harvest of which He is the firstfruit. The order is clear: "For since by man came death, by Man also came the resurrection of the dead. For as in Adam all die, even so in Christ all shall be made alive. But each one in his own order: Christ the firstfruits, afterward those who are Christ's at His coming. Then comes the end, when He delivers the kingdom to God the Father, when He puts an end to all rule and all authority and power. For He must reign till He has put all enemies under His feet. The last enemy that will be destroyed is death" (1 Corinthians 15:21-26). What this means to us is that Christ has won and we shall win. Death has no power over us in this interim period between Christ's first and second coming. Physical death is still a part of our future, but it has been stripped of its powers—

the symbols of its authority have been ripped away. We can say with Luther, "The body they may kill, but Thy truth abideth still," and with Athanasius, "The risen Christ makes life into a constant celebration."

In our conversation in this chapter, we have gone through the narrow tunnel of considering what life would be without the resurrection. We have come through the darkness, out into the sunshine of a new day for all of us. We have dared to ask, "If there is no resurrection, then what?" And we found the rugged reality that without the resurrection there would be:

No plan—Our God would not be in ultimate control.

No promise—Our gospel would be empty.

No power—Our faith would be aimless wishing.

No pardon—Our sins would still stain our souls.

No peace—Our fear of the future would rob us of the joy of living.

No purpose—Our life would be a cul-de-sac with no exit.

And so we sing with the early church the first Christian hymn: "Death, not Christ, died yesternight." And then we join with the saints around the throne of God in heaven and sing, "Hallelujah! The Lord God omnipotent reigneth!"

Then Jesus' words are whispered in our apprehensive hearts as we face life's impossibilities: "With man it is impossible, but with God nothing is impossible. I have come that you might have life and have it abundantly. Because I live, you shall live also. Now and forever." We can have a future without worry!

8

The Gift of Wisdom

Wisdom is the special gift of the Lord for our quest to know His will. It is beyond intellect and knowledge. In a willing mind, wisdom enables a person to hear with God's ears and see with His eyes. Wisdom is inspired depth-perception into people and situations. It is the vertical thrust of the mind of God into our minds, making discernment possible on the horizontal level of human affairs. With wisdom we can penetrate the mysteries of God—His nature, plan, and purpose.

Life is an endless succession of choices and decisions. We are called on to evaluate, analyze, and come to conclusions about what is right and best. The possibility of error for most of us is great. We look back at wrong choices and bad decisions. Some of them have taken us out of the mainstream of God's purpose. If we long to know God's maximum for our lives, wisdom is the gift we need and want in order to do the will of God.

I want to consider this gift of wisdom with you. To do that, we need to go back to Solomon and consider this endowment which became synonymous with his name and life. He was given an insight which draws us to an even greater wisdom in Christ and prepares us to appreciate and receive the gift through His Spirit. This is strategic for becoming a riverbed for the flow of guidance in our lives for the responsibilities we are given as well as the challenges we become willing to grasp.

When young King Solomon succeeded his father David as king of Israel, he felt acutely the impossible challenge of measuring up to his father and being the quality of king that his people needed. He had observed that his father David had a heart "after God's heart," and he observed the blessing that God gave David in the awesome task of leadership. The immense possibilities and grave dangers motivated the young man to long for God's power for his responsibilities. Along with the priests, he went to Gibeon, six miles north of Jerusalem, to make sacrifices to God where the Tabernacle stood. First Kings 3:4 tells us that he made a thousand burnt offerings on the altar. He was taking no chances: He needed and wanted God's blessing and power. When the sacrifices were completed, Solomon returned to his tent to sleep.

It was in a dream that the Lord appeared to Solomon's ready mind. In response to the king's desire for His help, the Lord made a propitious offer: "Ask! What shall I give you?"

How would you have answered? If you could make one wish for your own quest to know and do God's will, what would it be? What one gift from the Almighty would you ask for that would make everything else you need a possibility? Our minds dart to our immediate needs today. Then we wonder—what gift could we ask for that would provide everything else we need? Narrowing it down to one gift forces us to consider what is God's greatest gift—the one we need most and the one He longs most to give.

Solomon made his reply carefully. He began with praise to God for the amazing way He had empowered his father David. He remembered the secret of David's ready heart and the lovingkindness that God had provided in response. Then Solomon confessed his own inadequacy and need for strength to grasp the challenge of being king. This was followed by gratitude for the people over whom he was called to rule. Humility pulsated through his words. Only then did he dare to respond to God's offer. He asked for an "understanding heart." He wanted a heart capable of judging God's people and able to discern between good and evil. The Hebrew words translated "understanding heart" really mean a "hearing heart." Solomon wanted to be able to hear both God's voice and the people's needs, and to be able to speak to those needs out of the depth of the perception of God.

Solomon's request was in keeping with the custom of the time. When a matter of faith or practice needed a decision, it was customary to seek a word from the Lord through a priest, a prophet, or the king. The answer was given in either a *mishpāt*, a judgment on the basis of precedent, or a *tórāh*, a direct word from the Lord. In Solomon's response to the Lord's offer, he asked to have a hearing heart to discern what was right. The Hebrew means "to learn and obey" (*mishpāt*). The Lord's gracious reply seems to carry the assurance of both *mishpāt* and *tórāh*, precedent and direct word, coupled in an even greater gift. The Lord always gives us more than what we ask when we ask with humble receptivity and a desire to be effective in doing His will.

What Solomon asked for was pleasing to God. "Because you have asked for this thing," God told him, "and have not asked long life for yourself, nor have asked riches for yourself, nor have asked the life of your enemies, but have asked for yourself understanding to discern justice, behold, I have done according to your words; see, I have given you a wise and understanding heart, so that there has not been anyone like you before you, nor shall any like you arise after you" (1 Kings 3:11,12). *God promised to give Solomon the gift of wisdom.* He was faithful to that promise. Solomon became known for his wisdom. His life expressed it; so did his writings, sayings, and proverbs.

Have you noticed how God follows a gift with the opportunity to use it? That is so that we will know the power we have been given. Using the gift is part of the endowment. All God's gifts are for ministry, not just for our private enjoyment. God followed His promise of wisdom by putting Solomon in a situation in which both he and all of Israel would know that the gift had been given.

Two women came to him asking for his judgment on who was the rightful mother of a child. Both women had had a child. One child died. Now each claimed the remaining child as her own. Utilizing God's gift of wisdom, Solomon asked for a sword. "I will cut the child in half and give half to each of you!" Then the woman who was the real mother cried out in anguish, "O my lord, give her the living child, and by no means kill him!" The mother who had lied, saying the child was hers, said to be real mother, "Let him be neither mine nor yours, but divide him!"

Solomon's wise test had exposed the truth. "Give the first woman the living child, and by no means kill him. She is his mother." Instead of spending months listening to the wrangling mothers presenting their case, the king used God's gift of wisdom and exposed the truth. All were amazed at his divinely entrusted capacity. First Kings 3:28 reveals what that did to establish Solomon as the anointed one of God as King of Israel. "When Israel heard of the judgment which the king handed down, they feared the king; for they saw that the wisdom of God was in him to administer justice."

With the gift of wisdom, Solomon grew in power and greatness. He solidified the kingdom, expanded the frontiers of Israel's might, built a magnificent temple for the Lord, and became famous in the then-known world for his insight and sayings of truth. The Queen of Sheba came to learn from him. She tested him with difficult questions. Solomon answered each with divinely inspired wisdom. Her accolade stands as a testimony of the king's fame: "It was a true report which I heard in my own land about your words and your wisdom . . . Blessed be the Lord your God, who delighted in you, setting you on the throne of Israel! Because the Lord has loved Israel forever, therefore He made you king, to do justice and righteousness" (1 Kings 10:6,9).

To be sure, there are dark hours of disobedience in contrast to the bright splashes of glory in Solomon's portrait in Scripture. It is an awesome warning that no gift, not even the ultimate gift of wisdom, can be misused or fragmented from a faithful relationship to the Giver expressed in obedience. The gift and the Giver are one. The continuous flow of the gift of wisdom is dependent on fellowship and faithfulness to the daily, moment-by-moment guidance of the Source.

And yet, acknowledging Solomon's lack of using his gift in later years must not diminish our appreciation of what the gift accomplished at the height of his productivity. Solomon is distinguished not just for his judgments or his brilliant leadership, but for one particular God-given truth—that wisdom is the creative energy of God through which all things were made. He speaks of wisdom as John later spoke of the divine *Logos*. In his proverbs Solomon says, "The Lord by wisdom founded the earth; by understanding He established the heavens" (Proverbs 3:19). Wisdom for Solomon was the preexistent power through which (Whom!) He created and founded the world and humankind to be His people. The great king came very close to perceiving the essential trinitarian nature of God as Creator, Redeemer, and infilling Spirit of His people. And he discovered something more: The mysterious power of the mind of God could be received by a person who asked and trusted Him for it. The secret of receiving wisdom is to "trust in the Lord with all your heart, and lean not on your own understanding; in all your ways acknowledge Him, and He shall direct your paths. Do not be wise in your own eyes; fear the Lord and depart from evil" (Proverbs 3:5-7).

The same capacity of wisdom is offered you and me as we seek to know and do God's will. But true wisdom is not the prize of a lifetime search. We can chart the intellectual history of humankind's quest for understanding the riddle of life; the great religions, mystery religions, and philosophical schools of thought are all attempts to pierce the darkness of ignorance which have led to the knowledge of many facts, but too little wisdom about the cosmic meaning of the facts for living the abundant life.

An in-depth study of Solomon's life and learning still leads us to a thick curtain of mystery separating us with all our knowledge from the true perception of truth and reality. The wise sayings of Solomon become frustrating if we acknowledge their truth without having the will to live by them. The gift of wisdom given to the king was a foretaste of what God would do when He became incarnate as Wisdom Himself in Jesus Christ. We can grasp something of the truth if we word the Apostle John's familiar prologue, "In the beginning was Wisdom, and Wisdom was with God, and Wisdom was God. He was in the beginning with God. All things came into being by Him, and apart from Him nothing came into being that has come into being. In Him was life, and the life was the light of men. And the light shines in the darkness, and the darkness did not comprehend it." And Paul caught the full significance of the wonder: "Christ the power of God and the wisdom of God" (1 Corinthians 1:24).

Jesus referred to Himself as "a greater than Solomon." Christ was Wisdom Incarnate. And yet, people resisted the splendor of Wisdom's radiance. No wonder Jesus said, "The queen of the South [Queen of Sheba] will rise up in the judgment with the men of this generation and condemn them, for she came from the ends of the earth to hear the wisdom of Solomon; and indeed a greater than Solomon is here" (Luke 11:31). Solomon had gone as far as any human being in experiencing the precious gift of wisdom. Now here is Christ saying that what made the king great, and what was sought after by the leaders of His own time, was present with them. All that Jesus taught about God, the kingdom, and the ultimate purpose of life came out of the limitless storehouse of wisdom which He had with God before the foundation of the world.

For us today, in the confusing complications of living in the twentieth century, this means that in Christ we can receive, experience, and communicate the depth perception of true wisdom. Christ was, and now is, the power of God utilized to accomplish His ultimate purpose to create a people whom He loves and who will love Him. When we receive Christ, we receive wisdom. Then we are given the power to marshal thought and knowledge in the obedient service of accomplishing our true purpose: to seek and put first the kingdom of God and His righteousness, and to do His will. Wisdom indwelling in us integrates knowledge and guides our decisions. The ultimate choice of making Christ Lord of our lives is followed by a million choices in daily life which are guided by what will further our ultimate purpose: to live in fellowship with Him forever.

We do not need to wander aimlessly through life, uncertain and confused. We know whose we are and for what we were created. Our purpose is to know and do Wisdom's will. Whatever we discover of the nature of the universe can now be guided by our ultimate destiny. Wisdom grows in us as we grow in Christ. The facts of our scientific discoveries and the insight of our philosophic investigation become the raw material of the higher disciplines of discipleship. The crisis of our time of history is caused by the lack of wisdom among our thinkers, scientists, political leaders, and religious sages. We have more knowledge of the universe than ever before; we have penetrated the secret recesses of nuclear power; we have profound understanding of both the physiology and psychology of the human species. Only wisdom can unify all of that to make it a servant of progress. Without wisdom, our accumulation of intelligence leads us away from our purpose in life rather than closer to it.

That's the plight Paul experienced in the scholars of Athens. He tried to meet them on their own ground of intellectual philosophy. When he preached Christ and the power of the resurrection, they scoffed at the apostle. He left discouraged and alarmed by the evidence of knowledge undisciplined by wisdom. Paul's continued encounters with the Jewish authorities deepened his dismay. They wanted a display of God's power. The record of what Paul thought and felt after his confrontation with Athens' intelligence and Israel's religious establishments is eloquently preserved for us in the first two chapters of 1 Corinthians. His mind was on true wisdom, the wisdom of God in Christ, which both Jews and Greeks had rejected. What Paul wrote gives us a clear distinction between the wisdom of the world and the wisdom of God.

The apostle exposed the inadequacy of the passion of the Greeks for wisdom and the pertinacity of the Jews for evidence of God's power. "For Jews request a sign, and Greeks seek after wisdom" (1 Corinthians 1:22). In essence, each wanted assurance of the truth about God. This, Paul asserts, is to be found only in Christ crucified. The Jews stumbled over that offer of grace because it cut the taproot of the arrogance of self-justification. The Greeks called it foolishness, because it cut through the labyrinth of human speculative thought.

The answer to the quest for signs of intervention and for the wisdom of interpretation is revealed in Christ, who is the Power of God and the Wisdom of God. In essence, the brilliant apostle was inspired by Wisdom Himself to declare that God used all power in heaven and earth to accomplish the cosmic reconciliation of the world. God's greatest sign, the cross, was and is the revelation of ultimate wisdom. Instead of all the temporary measures He could have utilized, He made His big move on Calvary for the atonement of mankind. Christ could have raised an army to defeat Rome, or He could have set up a new philosophical school in Athens. Instead, the One who held all the power in heaven and earth (for which the Jews longed) and who incarnated wisdom (for which the Greeks yearned) employed His power to accomplish the wisest act of history. Those of us who accept the cosmic accomplishment have both unlimited power and undiminishable wisdom. "But of Him you are in Christ Jesus, who was made to us wisdom from God—and righteousness and sanctification and redemption—that, as it is written, 'He who glories, let him glory in the Lord' " (1 Corinthians 1:30,31).

The personal side of Wisdom's great revelation on the cross is our realization of Him in our daily life. Just as Wisdom used power to accomplish the cosmic end, so too He will guide us in the use of the power of intelligence and will to accomplish a life which fulfills its destiny. This helps us recap what we've been discovering about the will of God.

The three words Paul uses to describe wisdom in action on the cross are righteousness, sanctification, and redemption. The power of God was utilized to make us right with Himself, to enable us to grow in that reconciled relationship, and to bring us back to the full value of our destiny by paying the price for our salvation through forgiveness. Our response is spelled out in our own cross. We surrender ourselves, die to impetuous self-willfulness, and are raised to live a new life. Wisdom's greatest choice is our commitment to Christ. Then each decision we make is to further that newfound righteousness in all of life. As each choice is made with the imputed wisdom He provides, we are sanctified more and more, which means being formed in the likeness of Christ Himself. The redemption which "purchased our salvation" becomes like a time-release capsule as we accept forgiveness from God and our forgiveness of ourselves and others as the only wise way to live.

To put it very practically, the three dimensions of wisdom help us to ask crucial questions when we sort out what is best for ourselves and others. When faced with life's choices, we ask, "Will it further a right relationship with the Lord? Will it enable me to grow in cross-oriented Christlikeness? Will it express gracious forgiveness, redeeming hostility and hatred, or will it sell back to evil a part of me that belongs to the Lord? In all, will this choice or decision or action move me forward to the person I am destined to be now and forever?" When we answer these questions honestly and act in accordance with clear-cut guidance from the Lord, we have used the power of intellect, knowledge of the facts, and perception of how each choice fits into His plan. Wisdom is using power in the service of our destiny.

Now we are ready to see how this works in our fellowship with the Lord. Paul goes on in the second chapter of 1 Corinthians to show how the mind of Christ, Wisdom, can be imputed into our minds. The mysteries of God are not the prize of human pursuit but the gift of the Spirit of Christ living in us. We have barely tasted what God has prepared for us. Paul quotes Isaiah in heightening our anticipation and appreciation of what can be ours in this portion of heaven we call life: "Eye has not seen, nor ear heard, nor have entered into the heart of man the things which God has prepared for those who love Him" (1 Corinthians 2:9, based on Isaiah 64:4). but we don't have to wait! Paul says, "God has revealed them to us through His

Spirit." He goes on to say that the Spirit intercedes between the mind of God and the mind of man, "that we might know the things that have been freely given to us by God." The apostle reaches a crescendo by asking and answering Isaiah's ancient, probing question: "Who has known the mind of the Lord, that he may instruct Him?" And then the triumphant answer: "But we have the mind of Christ."

We have come full circle. Christ is the preexistent Wisdom of God. We behold the glory of that Wisdom sublimely revealed on the cross. Now our wisdom is not just an effort to apply His message and the impact of the cross to our daily lives, but a consistent communion with Wisdom Himself. When we accept the gift of the mind of Christ, we have superhuman perception; we share in Christ's character and disposition, and have an X-ray discernment of the implications of each decision for our forward movement toward what Paul called "the goal for the prize of the upward call of God in Christ Jesus" (Philippians 3:14).

No consideration of the magnificent gift of wisdom through the mind of Christ would be complete without a recognition of the source in the anointing and baptism of the Holy Spirit. In 1 Corinthians 12:8 Paul identifies the "word of wisdom" as one of the primary gifts of the Holy Spirit. Here "word" is congealed expression of what has been imputed in our mind. It is inspired thought put into expression. We can speak with heavenly wisdom. Our decisions will be in keeping with Christ's purpose for us; our insights for ourselves and others will be divinely infused with extraordinary discernment. We will have a "hearing heart," able to hear what the Spirit is saying and able to discern what people are expressing beneath what they are saying. And the gift is available to all of us—young and old, cultured and uncultured, those with a high I.Q. and those less intellectually endowed, the philosopher and the clerk, the scientist and the laborer, the pastor and the layman. We need not stumble through life, leaving behind us the shambles of inept or wrong choices. The Lord can make us wise.

Allow me to share a personal experience that I hinted about earlier. In the first few years of my Christian life I realized that though I knew Christ as my Lord and Savior, I was out of sync with Him. I bungled along doing the best I could with my innate intellectual ability. Decisions were arduous and often missed the mark. Counseling with people in spiritual need was long and exhausting. Then God led me to an in-depth study of the gifts of His Spirit. I studied the lives of great Christians in history who seemed to display a quality of wisdom in their relationships and their communication in writing and speaking. Without exception, each of those giants of the faith had gone through a pride-shattering realization of their own inadequacy, coupled with a plea that the wisdom gift of the mind of Christ be given them. Following their example, I asked a few trusted friends to come together to lay hands on me, asking God to entrust to me the gift of wisdom. That day was one of the most crucial transitions in my life. God answered my longing for a "hearing heart." Over the years I have experienced the results in more right decisions, deeper perception of people's needs, and greater precision in speaking truth with love and wisdom.

It is not blasphemy to be able to say of us that "a greater than Solomon is here." When Christ takes up residence in us and infuses His wisdom into us, we can tower over Solomon in all his glory! It all begins when we ask for what he asked—a hearing heart. But now on this side of Calvary and Pentecost, what God offers in response is all the practical wisdom He gave to Solomon *and* the fullness of wisdom incarnate in Christ now offered in His indwelling Spirit. He says longingly, "Ask what you wish Me to give you." Go for it! Ask for the mind of Christ, Wisdom—and everything else of any ultimate value will be yours as well!

9

A Secret for Specific Guidance

The title of this chapter holds out the promise of a sure way to know God's guidance in specifics. You may have responded, "Finally! I thought you'd never get around to it!" That's exactly what I want to do, though not in the steps of getting guidance, but rather in a quality of response to the Lord which makes those steps a possibility. In the next chapter I want to list five of the ways we can be more sure of the Lord's personal will for us. But before we do that, there is a gift we can give to God which prepares us to receive His gift of guidance in particulars. It is our gift of praise. There is a mighty power in praise which unlocks the secret of guidance.

We said that God is more ready to guide us than we are to be guided. Then we concluded from Scripture that God moves within us to free us to will to do His will. The sure sign that the sovereign will of God has energized our will is that we are overwhelmed with an uncontainable praise for Him and all He has done for us. That praise is also a releasing of our tight control over our own affairs. When we praise the Lord not only for what He *has done* but also for what he is *going to do,* something very significant happens to our will: we become open to possibilities that had never occurred to us before.

So the strategy for receiving specific guidance is praise! When we are in a tight spot, not knowing what to do, we need to praise God for the very thing which is causing our tension or pressure. If we are perplexed about the Lord's guidance in a relationship, we need to praise him for that difficult person. Whenever we face a problem which resists solution, we need to praise God for that perplexity. The moment a really impossible complexity hits, where whatever we do seems less than maximum, we need to praise God. At those crossroads in our lives when momentous decisions must be made and we fear going the wrong way, we need to praise God. When we do, a mysterious thing begins to happen: Consistent praise over a period of time conditions us to receive what the Lord has been waiting patiently to reveal to us or release for us.

In what I believe was Paul's earliest epistle, he gives us a powerful one-liner about the secret of knowing the will of God. In 1 Thessalonians 5:16-18 he said, "Rejoice always, pray without ceasing, in everything give thanks; for this is the will of God in Christ Jesus for you." If we are looking for a specific thing we are to do in order to know the will of God, here it is. It carries the impact of the seasoned experience of the apostle and the authority of Scripture. But, in addition to that, it has been tested over 2000 years of Christian history, and the great women and men of every age have found it works.

Thanks and praise in everything? "Paul, you've got to be kidding!" is our natural response. We recoil at the admonition that we should praise God in all the difficult and painful circumstances of our life. Ask God for strength to endure, surely, but praise Him in our complexities? Sickness, hurting relationships? Failure and frustration? Paul's word does not budge. There it stands, mocking us at first, and then intriguing us with an invitation to a totally different way of finding out what God may be saying to us in our difficulties and hard choices. We pause for a moment and stop ramming our wills against that immovable challenge; some very important things begin to dawn on us.

The first is that praise is both a response to God's greatness and goodness, and the ultimate level of relinquished trust. If we can praise God for what has happened to or around us, we are acknowledging that He can use *everything*. Praising God is affirming for ourselves His sovereignty and providence. The word "rejoice" is found over 20 times in Paul's epistles. In his letter to the Thessalonians, the word "always" is used four other times in addition to the admonition to rejoice always. It means all the time, on every occasion, in every set of circumstances. Colossians 1:24 is evidence that Paul took his own advice. Expressing his concern for the Colossians, he said, "I now rejoice in my sufferings for you, and fill up in my flesh what is lacking in the afflictions of Christ, for the sake of His body, which is the church." He gave praise for the anguish he was going through over their problems of living faithfully in spite of the spiritual distractions of heresies and moral laxity in the Colossian church. But his praise was in a greater perspective. He was able to be involved in the extension of the cross in that and many other situations. "What is lacking" does not mean deficiency in the atoning cross of Christ, but the unfinished task of living it out and bringing its power to everyone. That had gotten him into a lot of troubles, heartaches, and suffering. I think that rejoicing had made the Lord's will clear and had made Paul willing to do what he was called to do.

The apostle's personal experience of the power of praise was also the basis of sounding the trumpet call to adoration with the Philippians. They too had problems inside the church and from hostile forces outside the fellowship. "Rejoice in the Lord always. Again I say, rejoice!" Catch the qualifying note "in the Lord." He's not talking about a surface giddiness. The rejoicing is to be in fellowship with the Lord, to the Lord, and for the Lord. Rejoicing in the Lord gives His perspective on things and His power to know what we are to do.

But does this thing really work? From years of experience trying it, I can say an enthusiastic "yes!" Whenever I say in prayer, "Lord, I don't understand what You are doing in this, but I praise You for it," a tight tenseness inside me relaxes. And I don't have to go back years, months, or weeks to illustrate it. It happened this morning.

I am writing this book during my summer study leave. But it's one of the three major projects which must be completed by the end of this summer. In addition, I'd be less than a concerned Pastor of my people if I didn't bring with me long prayer lists of people about whom I am deeply concerned. Pile on that the normal administrative and financial demands of running a big church which no amount of geographical distance allows a responsible leader to forget. Then multiply all that by the challenges of a growing television ministry, and you have more than enough to occupy a prolonged morning prayer time. For a moment as I began my intercessory and supplicating prayers for people and situations, I felt bogged down. My prayers seemed perfunctory. So I remained quiet for a time. The thought invaded my mind and created a desire which followed in an act of will. "Why not praise Me?" the Lord seemed to be saying. "But I already prayed the general prayers of praise and thanksgiving at the opening of my prayer time," I responded in thought. And the answer: "Make all of your prayers for people and problems praise this morning." I followed orders. As I prayed specifically for each one of my concerns, praising the Lord for them, I got an immediate release. In some complex situations where I had to make some important decisions, praise freed my mind to think new thoughts and feel a fresh desire to follow the leading I received. I arose from my knees refreshed and confident.

I had to laugh out loud when I sat down to write. The outline of this book had been planned months before. I opened my writing pad and saw the theme of this chapter and all the notes I had gathered to incorporate in it. The power of praise! I had just been through a personal rediscovery of that power. The fresh discovery gave me gusto to continue our discussion of the will of the Lord by unfolding this open secret given to us by the Apostle Paul.

But you may be thinking "that's not suffering or excruciating data you released to God in praise that morning." True, but I was feeling pressured and bogged down. You feel that way at times too, don't you? Too much to do with self-imposed deadlines, people concerns, unresolved problems, decisions to make. Do you ever find that attention to one thing in your mind is distracted by all the others? Of course you do. Praise is the key to taking them one at a time and receiving clear guidance.

Just in case you're still not sure I've tested this Scripture in really tough things, allow me to share a few. Any leader has his cheering section plus a few people who feel divinely appointed to help him or her grow by frustrating what he or she is trying to do. As a strong-willed person, I'm not always right, but I'm seldom unsure of my goals.

In a basic decision about the direction of a church in which I was serving some years ago, I locked horns with a church officer who was outspokenly opposed. (The specific details are avoided purposely to "protect the innocent" and to free you to make a personal application from your own life.) The conflict became a personal issue for both the officer and me. Neither of us wanted to lose. If I lost, it would have crippled my future leadership; if he lost, he would also lose face with people he had rallied to his cause. Late one night, sleepless with concern over the situation, I paced my bedroom floor, trying to convince God of how "right" I was and how dangerous this man was to the kingdom's growth in that church. "Simply praise Me for this man and for the no-win situation you've gotten yourself into," was the only guidance I got. I spent the rest of the night doing that.

By morning I had a strange, mysterious feeling of release from the situation. What I thought was the prelude to Armageddon was just one phase in God's strategy for that church. And to my surprise, I felt very differently about that church officer! For the first time in that long ordeal I asked, "I wonder where I missed with him? Why had I not followed my basic conviction of leadership that people can support only those things they share in developing?" I believe that a church can move no farther or faster than the officers' experience of the truth behind the direction they want for their church. That made me want to reel back and include the man in the vision, and more than that, allow him to help shape the vision. After all, it *was* his church too! I felt an urge to call him and ask to see him. That was submerged in the equivocation that he wouldn't respond and would see it as the first stage of his victory in the conflict.

But someone else had been awake all that night. The man's wife. She had taken seriously a sermon I had preached on praising the Lord as the key to unlocking difficulties. (Some sermons are preached before the preacher has lived his own convictions!) She had practiced what I preached by praising God for what we were all going through. That prompted her to follow the good-morning coffee she served her husband with the suggestion, "Why not call Lloyd, share your real feelings of not being consulted, and tell him you want what God wants, which *may* be better than what either of you thinks is His will?" Praising the Lord had not only given her that gift of wisdom, but had prompted a willingness in the man's heart to find a solution. He didn't know why, but he was open to her suggestion. She knew why!

As I was putting off calling the man, the phone rang. A reserved but pleasant voice said, "I think we need to talk. Do you have an opening in your schedule today?" Did I! My positive response led to the first of many talks and a final decision which was a victory for neither of us, but for the peace and unity of the church, as well as its forward movement. And praise had done it! I have returned to the lessons learned about rejoicing in that situation many times over the years.

In the area of facing illness in my family, when my wife was undergoing cancer treatment, the deeper freedom to trust God with the future came to us when we could praise God however it turned out. Our lives and our marriage were deepened immeasurably through it.

Like any father, I've been through my share of concerns for my children. All three have become great people in spite of those times of crisis when their growing up forced me to grow in grace. Here again, praise for the problems was the only way I made it through. Each challenge finally brought me back to the secret of rejoicing in the midst of unsolved problems which were turned into milestones of character development for all of us at the turning point of praise.

Each of the major turning points in my life brought me to further realization of the power of praise. Times of insecurity or challenge too big for my talents were unlocked when I thanked God for what I was going through. And it's not over. The future will be filled with life's fine blend of ups and downs. My only prayer is that I will be able to remember to praise Him sooner. I could fill a book with specific examples from my own life of the rediscovery that praise is the will of God for us, through which we learn the specifics of that will.

It is also one of the most effective ways of helping people find release and guidance. When I am privileged to be trusted with the intimate problems of people in friendship conversations or counseling, I find that after talking and sharing, helping them praise the Lord enables a liberating release. Praise helps people let go and realize that the Lord has power available to help them. When praise begins, the needed guidance comes. Marriages can be reconciled, bodies healed, conflicts resolved, solutions found, and next steps in God's strategy realized.

That leads us to the second part of the blessing we receive in always praising the Lord. Paul's startling admonition calls us not only to rejoice, but to rejoice in advance of a solution or resolution. I find that this is the time when our imagination comes into active participation with the will. Praising the Lord makes us willing and releases our imaginations to be used by Him to form the picture of what He is seeking to accomplish. A resistant will makes us very uncreative and lacking in adventuresome vision in the use of our capacity of imagination. God wants to use our imagination in the painting of the picture of what He is leading us to dare to hope for and expect. Once the picture becomes clearer to us, we will find that the will is a wonderful administrator of our energy to accomplish a task with the Lord's help. We become what we envision under the Spirit's guidance. That's why our own image of ourselves, other people, our goals, and our projects all need the inspiration of our imagination. However, until the Holy Spirit begins His work releasing it, our will keeps our imagination stunted and immature.

Consistent, daily, hourly prayers of praise make the difference. That's why Paul stresses rejoicing always, praying without ceasing, and giving thanks in everything. All of life is to be bathed in praise. This provides the Lord with what I call creative lead-time. Our praise, as the ultimate level of relinquishment, allows Him to get us ready for the decisions we must make or the next steps He wants us to take. He knows what's ahead of us and wants us to live in the flow of a constant companionship in which He can engender the wisdom we will need.

Taking advantage of creative lead-time can be a source of unpressured freedom from panic for us. So often, we put off talking to the Lord about a problem until the crisis deadline. We muddle with the concern, and then when the decision or choice must be made, we burst into His presence, and want an immediate answer. Consistent fellowship with Him could have made that unnecessary. To be sure, there are emergencies which arise for which we need special guidance, but that can be received much more readily when we've been spending time in praise on a faithful, daily, hourly basis. And in the choices and decisions we know are ahead, praising God for them immediately and then waiting for the conditioning of communion with Him, enables us to be sure of His will in our lives.

Lead-time becomes very creative when we wait patiently for God. When a difficult problem must be solved or a hard choice must be made, tell the Lord about it, praise Him for it, and then put off the resolution until He has had full access to your mind and imagination. After the initial praise, thank Him constantly that the answer is on the way, and that in time and on time, you will know what He wants you to do.

A woman came to see me about her "unsolvable problems." She said she wanted God's will for her life. When we got into the specific problems, she confessed that she did not know how to pray. We talked through the potential of praise for each of the needs. She started experimenting with a kind of "release through rejoicing" prayer therapy. She is a competent executive with a large company. Her thoroughness and attention to detail were utilized in keeping a log which has become a kind of spiritual autobiography. She kept track of problems surrendered with praise. The amazing thing to her was the new freedom to imagine solutions to the very problems that had brought her to see me. In a time of prayer with her, we asked for the anointing of the Holy Spirit on her will and imagination. She became willing and imaginative. Many of the problems were solved by receiving and willing the Lord's "picture" of the answer.

Other problems she has endured with patience, waiting for the Lord's timing. Like all of us, she's in the process, and the Lord is not finished with the person He intends her to be. But through praise, she is ready and willing, knowing that the best is still out ahead.

Rejoice always, Paul? Yes, always. In everything give thanks? Yes! It is God's will that this is the way we know His will.

10

Five Steps to Be Sure of God's Personal Will

Henry Drummond once said, "There is a will of God for me which is willed for no one else besides. It is a particular will for me, different from the will He has for anyone else—a private will—a will which no one else knows about, which no one can know but me."

By the use of the word "private," the great Drummond did not mean that the will of God for each of us is separatistic, freeing us from responsibility for others. What he explains is that as a part of the eternal purpose of God, He has a personal will for each of us which is His plan for us as individuals.

Knowing God's personal will is the thrust of this concluding chapter. God knows and cares about each of us individually and uniquely. We can learn a great deal about the basic principles of knowing God's will from others, but finally our attention must turn to that special person who lives in our skin.

That involves five great friendships which are all part of the one great friendship with God for which we were born. In the context of these friendships, we can take five steps of pivoting our will into God's will. When the ultimate will of God becomes our unerring chart, then we are able to take our own personal voyage according to the particular plan He makes known in these friendships. Our gracious and loving Lord has a personal plan for each of us, our own way of living out His essential will that we know, love, glorify, and serve Him.

Each of these friendships is His idea. He gives them to us. They are not a substitute for knowing and doing His will, but the way He helps us when we desire the working out of His plan for our lives. They are offered to us in the light of everything we've said thus far.

A recap may be helpful. God has chosen and called us. His Spirit has been at work within us, calling us out of the bondage of the wrong idea of freedom. He has helped us see that free will ends up in the prison of self-centeredness and lack of resoluteness. Our will is not really free until He sets it free. But we have been elected by Him to know His will. That will is Jesus Christ—life in Him and His life in us. By supernatural power we were given the gift of faith to receive Christ as Savior and Lord. He has made us willing to be made willing to receive all that He did for us in the cross, the resurrection, and Pentecost. Christ abiding in us and our abiding in Him has begun to transform our mind around His mind. A Christ-controlled thought life has brought our brain to be His ready servant. His acceptance and forgiveness now is beginning to be the dominant thought of the cerebral cortex of our brain. Our will is being triggered to marshal all our resources in obedient discipleship for the One who loves us and gave His life for us. We are no longer our own private possession. He is the purpose and passion of our life. Our drives have been congealed; our will for our life is to know and do His personal will for us. He has become both our sovereign Lord and our personal Friend.

The first great friend that He introduces to us as a part of loving and knowing Him is His Word, the Bible. Consistent, daily reading of the Bible prepares us for each step of His evolving plan for us. He inspired the writing of it so that we could have an objective standard for knowing what He wants us to do. The first two questions and answers of the Westminster Shorter Catechism show us why the Bible is so important in receiving guidance. What is the chief end of man? "Man's chief end is to glorify God and to enjoy Him forever."

"What rule has God given to show us how we may glorify and enjoy Him?" "The Word of God, which is contained in the Scriptures of the Old and New Testaments, is the only rule to direct us as to how we may glorify and enjoy Him." If we are serious about knowing God's plan, we will listen to what He has to say in the Bible.

But that takes more than what I call a "lucky dip" into the Bible. That's going to the Bible at a time of crisis or decision-making and hoping we can find specific direction. It's allowing the Bible to fall open to any page, closing our eyes, and putting our finger on a particular verse as the instruction of God. The often-quoted story of the man who wanted quick guidance from the Bible is a good example of this. He let the Bible fall open and put his finger on the verse "Judas went out and hanged himself." That was not the guidance he wanted, so he made another attempt. This time his finger landed on the verse "Go thou and do likewise." That shook him up, so he made one further "lucky dip." The verse his finger fell on this time was "And what thou doest, do quickly." A rather unlucky dip, I'd say, especially if he had been an emotionally disturbed person with a suicidal death wish.

No less a scholar and preacher than John Wesley found that opening the Bible at random can be less than effective. When he was trying to make the decision of whether to assist George Whitefield in evangelizing the inmates at Bristol Prison, he randomly opened the Bible and read, "And devout men carried Stephen to his burial." A Moravian friend tried it for him and opened on this verse: "And Ahaz slept with his fathers." Wesley knew some very powerful verses he could have turned to which leave little question about the Christian's duty to minister to the lost and lonely and imprisoned as specifically admonished by Jesus in Matthew 25. However, on May 24, 1738, the day when Wesley's heart was "strangely warmed" and the Spirit of God set him free to become one of the great preachers of history, that morning he had opened his Bible and read, "Thou art not far from the kingdom of God." There the passage was in confirmation of a growing need for the Holy Spirit in his life and what the Lord had been telling him and preparing him to receive. The point is that God will use the Bible as a part of consistent, daily study of His Word. Panic plunges are dangerous.

But by far the greatest value of concentrated study of the Bible is that it engenders in our thinking the whole counsel of the Lord about Himself and our relationship with Him. In the Bible we have the unfolding revelation of the will of God and the accounts of people like you and me who struggled, responded, and sometimes resisted God's best for their lives. The Bible is an honest book depicting real people with authentic needs. Learning how to use it for guidance in the will of God is the crucial thing.

My suggestion is to begin daily reading in the New Testament. The whole Bible is an example of Hebrews 1:1,2: "God, who at various times and in different ways spoke in time past to the fathers by the prophets, has in these last days spoken to us by His Son, whom He has appointed heir of all things, through whom also He made the worlds." The Old Testament leads up to the incarnation; the Gospels describe the cosmic event, along with what Christ actually said about the will of God; Acts paints the dramatic portrait of the new humanity whose wills have been liberated to become women and men in Christ; the epistles spell out the implications for living this new life in Christ; and Revelation tells us how history will be culminated.

You may have been a faithful Bible student for years and read through the Bible many times. If not, I recommend beginning with Mark. It gives a fast-moving account of the life, message, death, and resurrection of Christ. Then go back and read Matthew. Before you start Matthew, take a week to read carefully Exodus 20 and Deuteronomy 5-8 to get the Ten Commandments clearly into your thinking. Now go through Matthew, taking a chapter a day. You may be surprised that I suggest next that you read Luke, another of the Gospels. The reason is that Christ is the Center and Source of the will of God. The more we know about what He said and the more we memorize actual passages about the will of God, the more prepared we will be to make our decisions in keeping with His ultimate will. Luke and Acts are companion books to be read consecutively. After you've finished Luke, go on to Acts.

Now we're ready for Paul and his epistles. Here's a helpful order: 1 and 2 Thessalonians, Philippians, Galatians, Ephesians, Colossians. Next tackle Romans. You will find that to be especially exciting in light of what you've read thus far. It is a comprehensive theological treatise on the will of God for our lives. After that you will be ready to appreciate the writings of John in a much more profound way. The Gospel of John, plus 1, 2, and 3 John, and then Revelation, were all written by the Apostle John, who was one of

Jesus' disciples. Read Revelation after you have read John's Gospel and epistles. After this you are ready to read all the other books of the New Testament.

When you've finished, I would suggest a daily trip through the Bible, beginning with Genesis and continuing all through the Old Testament and straight through the New Testament. Do it in a year. With morning and evening readings, that makes 730 segments. But don't make a fetish about how much you read each day. Figure out your own pace. If it takes two years or more, don't worry. But do it! The people I know who are clear about the will of God *and* daily guidance have made this a practice. You will find that you take decisions in stride with an inner assurance based on scriptural authority.

It is important to underline the fact that God speaks in different ways through His Word about His will, one way directly and the other way indirectly. Distinguishing is crucial. In His commandments and direct statements we are clearly told what His will is for us. In fact, they are the absolute standard of our faith and practice. When we are searching for the will of God, we can be very sure that it will not contradict the Ten Commandments. These are the basics to govern our lives in all times, places, and relationships. They are an expression of God's original and present will in our lives. Augustine was right in praying, "Grant that we may never seek to bend the straight to the crooked—that is, Thy will to ours—but that we may bend the crooked to the straight—that is, our will to Thine." We don't break the commandments; we break our lives on them when we deny them.

The same is true for all the sayings of Jesus. They carry the same authority as the Commandments and are part of the absolute standard for us. Knowing the will of God requires a commitment to read, memorize, and live what the Lord said. All that He says to us today will be built on it.

The teaching of the writers of the epistles makes those sayings applicable to our intellectual, moral, and social life. The promises about the will of God are immensely helpful in focusing our minds on Christ.

Now a statement about the indirect way God speaks to us. The Bible contains accounts of people whom He called and elected to know His will. What He said and did in their lives helps us discern His will for us. Though the circumstances differ, a basic principle of guidance emerges. For example, in the life of Gideon we witness the call and equipping of a frightened Israelite to be the courageous general of 300 men to defeat 132,000 Midianites. In the account we learn about God's clear commands to Gideon to be a leader. God gave him a step-by-step strategy of how to do it. Then, after this undeniable call and guidance, Gideon devised a test with a fleece to be sure. First he told God that he would put the fleece on the threshing floor, and said that if by morning there was dew on the fleece only but the ground around it was dry, he would know that he was to lead Israel against the Midianites. God met the worried leader's test. In the morning there was enough dew on the fleece to fill a bowl. That should have convinced him. But he asked for a repeat performance, except that this time he wanted the ground to be wet and the fleece dry! Again God responded to his need to be sure. The ground was wet and the fleece dry the next morning when Gideon awoke.

Does that mean that this passage about Gideon tells us that we are to devise our own fleece test? I don't think so. God had told Gideon His will. But Gideon was not willing to act in raw trust. Out of love for him, God helped him be sure.

Gideon's fleece test is not a biblical mandate for us. Nor is the demand for signs. What this account tells us is that God will use whatever is necessary to convince us that what He has already told us is true. God does not use our test to tell us about what He wants us to do. He may give us an assuring sign in confirmation of what He wants, but seldom one to introduce us to a phase of His will. Often when a conviction is growing in me through Bible study and prayer, I hear something said or observe something in situations around me which gives me an "Aha!" of confirmation. If that's all I went on to know the will of God, I'd be sailing with no chart, no compass, no sextant to read the stars, no radio for communication, and no Pilot aboard. All I would have to guide me would be my observation of the sea and the passing ships which may be heading for a different port!

We are told that the reason the Titanic hit and was sunk by the iceberg was that the ship's radios were completely jammed for hours before with silly "ship-to-shore" conversations of the passengers with friends and families in Britain and America. Other ships in the area were not able to get through with a warning signal. Repeating that story is a sign to me, confirming some guidance the Lord has been giving me lately. "Keep the lines open, Lloyd. Don't jam the communication lines of prayer with talk about what you need and want so that I can't get through to you." The Titanic story confirms a hundred or more passages in the Bible in which I have heard the same truth. The story was a confirmation, not an introduction, to the truth. Signs are helpful if they confirm what the Bible has been saying to us.

Another example of how God speaks indirectly in telling us how His will works is in the life of John Mark. When we read Paul's words to the Colossians about Mark, one sentence says so much about the transformation of a man and the healing of a broken relationship. In Colossians 4:10 Paul mentions that Mark is with him during his imprisonment in Rome, and then gives a parenthetical admonition that if Mark comes to Colosse, the Christians should receive him. The reinstatement of a failure! Mark was Barnabas' cousin. Paul and Barnabas had taken him on their first missionary journey, but he defected at Perga in Pamphylia. The young man became a missionary dropout. When it came time for the return visit to the churches in a second missionary journey, Barnabas wanted to take Mark along again, giving him a second chance. Paul vehemently disagreed. A rift was wedged between Paul and Barnabas over Mark. The result was that they split up and went in different directions. The Bible is honest about human relationships. It also tells about what can happen to heal them.

Mark was introduced to a deeper life in Christ, first by Barnabas and later by Peter. He became Peter's helper and companion. Peter knew about failure and the Lord's power to make possible new beginnings. He never forgot the cock's triple crow or Jesus' patient healing of his guilty heart beside the Sea of Galilee after the resurrection. So the apostle not only helped heal Mark's remorse over failure, but also rooted Mark's vascillating faith in the actual life and message of Christ. In the years together, Mark heard the truth through an eyewitness. With Peter he went to Rome and as a mature man in Christ was reconciled with Paul and brought him fellowship and comfort in prison. That's why Paul wanted to clear up the record about Mark with the church.

Mark, once a failure but now a strong disciple of Christ, took all that he had learned from Peter about the Savior's life, ministry, and actual words, and then, under the Spirit's inspiration, wrote the first Gospel to be written!

We lean back and think about what that has taught us about the will of God. His perfect and provisional will are demonstrated. The Lord's perfect will was that Mark become a fully mature person in Christ. Surely His plan for him was that he write his Gospel. But did the Lord cause his failure or the rift between Paul and Barnabas to get Mark into fellowship with Peter in preparation for writing his Gospel? Hardly. The Lord could have gotten Peter and Mark together without all that anguish and strife. What He did instead was to exercise His circumstantial will to accomplish His intentional will. The Lord wove the mistakes and failures into the tapestry of Mark's life and moved him on to get His work done. We are sure there were times when Mark wondered what the Lord was doing with him. We wonder if he looked back with praise, realizing what the Lord had done, not in spite of his earlier failure, but through it. Surely he must have, for only a man of great gratitude could have written the Gospel of Mark with such gusto and grace.

In both Gideon and Mark we have thought about what God says to us indirectly through passages of Scripture. What begins as indirect ends up very direct! The key is putting ourselves into passages and experiencing what really happened. Then we can ask, "Lord, what are You saying to me in this passage? How does this apply to my search to know and do Your will?" This is what Walter Russel Bowie called "seeing ourselves in the Bible."

One final and crucial word about our friendship with the Bible. The Holy Spirit is our guide and wisdom in reading it. He takes the words and applies them to our personal quest for the will and guidance of the Lord. He creates the desire to become immersed in the Word of God and is with us as Interpreter and Guide as we read.

The second friend the Lord gives us to know His personal will for our lives is prayer. I speak of communication with the Lord in prayer as a friend because it does for us what a great friend does: It affirms, strengthens, and lovingly corrects. And the friendship of prayer is God's special gift. It begins with Him. Don't ever lose sight of the fact that the desire to pray is because God wants to be in communication with us. Consistent morning-and-evening daily prayer is reporting in for an appointment that He has set. The willingness to be on time and ready both to listen and respond is the result of His desire to be with us. Imagine that! The Lord of the universe loves us so much that He wants to make His specific will clear to us. During the day, in between appointments, we will need to pray brief, flash prayers. Here again, before it was our idea to call out to Him, He gave us the willing thought. I think of it in this way: Between appointments, morning and evening, He sees that we may not have gotten our orders clearly. Or things emerged during the day which He knew were coming but which we wouldn't be able to really desire or appropriate His guidance about until we were in the thick of things. Those brief, on-the-job training instructions or insights are so that we can keep in touch with Master Control. When we think "I'd better pray about that!" it's because the Lord has first said, "I want you to pray. I am ready to give you something which I have reserved for this moment of crisis or opportunity."

But it's what happens in those longer times of silence, meditation, and response that counts for the development of our understanding of the personal will of God. I have discovered that these times at the beginning and end of each day are made maximum with adoration, confession, thanksgiving, meditation, intercession, supplication, and dedication. Here's how it works: Our conversation begins by adoring the Lord for who He is, what He has done in and around us, and what He means to us. That establishes His sovereignty over us and focuses His infinite love for us. On any particular day we may be filled with special adoration for an aspect of His nature which has become especially meaningful to us.

Now we are ready to confess our sins. Sin is anything which separates us from Him, ourselves, or any other human being. Also, many of the things we need to confess involve our calling as Christians in society. What are those things which we thought about but never did and those things which we did to contradict His love and guidance because we thought about them too little?

Thanksgiving is now centered on His forgiveness and the chance of a new beginning. Refusing to renew that grace with complete acceptance each day is a more serious sin than our other sins. Refreshed with overflowing gratitude, we are ready to spread out all the needs and concerns that we have for ourselves and others. Take time to listen to the Lord; wait quietly as He guides our thinking. This time of listening is crucial because it gives us the substance of what He wants us to ask for in our intercessory prayers for others and our supplication for ourselves.

Meditation is offering the Lord a willing mind that is ready to think His thoughts after Him and able to ask for what the time of quiet has clarified. As we discussed earlier, this kind of prayer gets us ready to know what He wants us to be and do when His timing has determined that it is best for us and all concerned. It immerses us in union with Christ, who is the focus of our released will and the One whose mind guides our mind.

Knowledge of the Lord's will and personal guidance usually doesn't happen overnight. That's why the lead time we referred to earlier is so important. Not for God, but for us.

God wants us to possess our possessions through prayer. Dedication is accepting what is ours. It is His will that we be filled with love (Romans 5:5). He wants us to live in His peace (Philippians 4:7). His will is that we have joy (Romans 15:13). And He wants to give us His Spirit (Acts 2:38,39; Ephesians 5:18). In our prayer, God does for us what He did for Abraham when He encouraged him to walk through the land He had promised him: "Arise, walk in the land through its length and its width; for I give it to you" (Genesis 13:17). Put that with Paul's exclamation, and there's reason to keep an appointment with God in prayer: "For all things are yours . . . the world or life or death, or things present or things to come—all are yours. And you are Christ's, and Christ is God's" (1 Corinthians 3:21b-23).

Prayer is not overcoming God's reluctance to guide us; it puts our wills in a condition to receive what He wills for us. It changes our moods and gives us keen desires.

At age 33, Charlotte Elliot, because of the pressure of musical education, had become a hopeless invalid. During this time she became bitter and rebellious. One evening she was visited by Dr. Cesar Malan, a Swiss minister and musician. In her frustration and despair she asked him how to become a Christian. His reply was simple: "You pray this prayer: 'O God, I come to You just as I am.' " This simple-worded prayer led to her life of faith and the writing of the hymn "Just As I Am" 14 years later. She also wrote this prayer which exemplified her trust:

> Renew my will from day to day;
> Blend it with Thine, and take away
> All now that makes it hard to say,
> "Thy will be done."

The next friend God gives us may surprise you. Ourselves! With the first two friends, Scripture and prayer, we can dare to begin to trust our thoughts and feelings. God gave us both intellect and emotions to cooperate with our will in doing His will. Without the fact of Scripture and a faith nurtured in prayer, our thoughts and feelings cannot be trusted. But when thought-controlled feelings follow both fact and faith, we can begin to use our gifts. We can pray with the Psalmist, "Teach me good judgment and knowledge, for I believe Your commandments" (Psalm 119:66). He is asking for the ability to understand and apply the commandments, so that when challenges arise he will be able to decide what direction to take. The original Hebrew word translated as "judgment" here is taám. It really means "taste." Derek Kidner says that this implies taste "not in an artistic judgment but of spiritual discrimination."* Job's friend Elihu said, "For the ear tests words as the palate tastes food" (Job 34:3). We have been given the capacity of discernment to be able to sort things out.

God trusts us more than we may trust the capabilities that He has given us. The thing I'm seeking to stress is that when our will is ready to do God's will because of the miracle of His release, we can be much more confident of our analysis of situations, thinking things through prayerfully, and making decisions and evaluations. If each morning we have asked for guidance, we should expect it to happen.

God probably will not send a dove down into our place of work or our church budget meeting with written instructions rolled up neatly and stuck in its beak. He expects us to do hard thinking and come to tough decisions. But exercising

---

*Derek Kidner, Psalms 73-150, Tyndale Old Testament Commentaries, general editor D.J. Wiseman (Inter-varsity Press, Leicester, England).

our intellectual capacity is based on claiming John's bold promise, "But you have an anointing from the Holy One, you know all things" (1 John 2:20). At least we know enough to ask for the anointing of the Spirit on all our thinking. The prayer *is* answered.

I think of a woman who served with me on a committee. We would begin each meeting of the group with a time of prayer, each person contributing in the supplication for God's will and guidance. When decisions had to be made, this woman could be counted on to interrupt just before the vote and say, "Are we sure we are doing God's will? Wouldn't it be better to put it off until we've had more time to pray?" At first we complied with her request, holding off things that needed to be decided for the expansion of the kingdom. But we all noticed that she was no more ready to be decisive after the delay. "Didn't we pray at the beginning of the meeting, and haven't we been praying all through the meeting?" a woman finally said in exasperation when the holding action was suggested one more time. There was no reply except a general statement with a barbed, guilt-producing hook in it: "Well, the problem with Christians today is that they do what they want and expect the Lord to bless it."

True. But the statement may have been a confession more than an analysis of unguided decisions. The more I came to know the woman, the more I understood her lack of self-esteem in Christ and her inability to appreciate how He could use the person she had been equipped to be.

Actually, she was a very intelligent person and had not accepted that her abilities for serving the Lord included her sensitivity *and* her high I.Q. They could be used for His glory. When He began to change her image of herself, she discovered new courage to use her gifts, allowing Him to guide the process of analysis of problems and alternative solutions. She realized that consistently refusing to make a decision was a decision!

So often Christian organizations muddle with the question, "Is this God's will or just human analysis?" Any decision is both. After we've done our homework in both Scripture and prayer, we can trust the Spirit of the Lord to guide a final decision. Consecrated thinking is a gift we give to the Lord. In response, He gives us His mind.

In our personal lives, prayerful thinking will lead us to insights and conclusions. Dare to trust the Lord in you!

When I was recently in Edinburgh, Scotland, I overheard a construction worker give a pointed challenge to a fellow worker. It might be a good motto for us in using our gifts of thinking and discernment in discovering God's guidance. "Use your head, mon, thinkin's not gone out of style!" And it's never out of style for Christians who have been on their knees and in their Bibles.

The same thing can be said for our feelings of rightness or wrongness about choices or decisions. Of course, they can be distorted by confused thinking, repressed anxieties, and unhealed prejudices. But when we make every effort to become honest, open people, God helps us bring our thinking in line with His kingdom purposes and shows us the inner tensions He wants to heal. He helps us in our prayers to deal with our hurts on a daily basis, and unpeels us like an onion, one layer at a time, until He has control of more and more of us. He wants to use our feelings in the service of His will. His goal is to make us people who feel inside that something is best or not maximum for us or others. When we feel strongly about something, it is good to check to see if the feeling contradicts what we know of God's will from study and prayer, as well as previous revelations from Him.

The way I've found best in approaching my feelings about things I am considering is to allow the feeling to be honored and experienced. Then I ask God to change the feeling if it's wrong or to make it even stronger if it's right.

Again, if the Lord abides in us and we abide in Him, He can guide our feelings. Consistently put your feelings at the disposal of the Lord. Then if you continue to have that inner feeling of something being wrong about a choice, don't do it! Also, when you feel positive and give the Lord a chance to change it, and if that "rightness" feeling persists, forge ahead!

Added to using our thoughts and trusting our feelings, we are encouraged to take a good look at our talents. These are the natural endowments the Lord has given us. Guidance in the Lord's personal will for us usually involves developing these talents to the maximum. He will lead us into situations and opportunities that help us grow in excellence. A good test of a decision or choice is whether it will stretch us in the next stage of the development of our talents.

But don't analyze your talents without also considering what the Lord offers you to augment your natural capabilities. The fruit of the Spirit, listed in Galatians 5:22,23, offers us the character of Christ to be engendered in our character. Look at the different kinds of fruit: love, joy, peace, patience, kindness, goodness, faithfulness, gentleness, self-control. Our talents are to be maximized by these character traits of the Master. He entrusts them to us. And His will for us as individuals usually involves leading us into situations where they will grow in us. We can be sure that He will not guide us to do anything which can be done without dependence on them or that would in any way contradict them. This is another good test of guidance.

Added to that, you and I are meant to be gifted people! That may surprise you. Our tendency is to think of gifted people as those who have spectacular human abilities. That's not what I am suggesting. In the New Testament we are told that there are special spiritual gifts given to us for our ministry with people and for our leadership in the church and the world. According to 1 Corinthians chapters 12 and 13, we can expect the Lord to lead us into opportunities where love, wisdom, knowledge, faith, healing, working of miracles, prophecy, and power to praise will be needed and provided.

The gifts are for all Christians. He gives them so that we can carry out our ministry to people with power beyond our own understanding and strength. For our responsibilities of leadership, He gives us wisdom and knowledge. When we care for people with His heart, He gives us faith to believe that all things are possible—to pray for healing and His miraculous interventions in people and circumstances. He endows us with His discernment to see beneath the surface of people and situations and to pray for spiritual liberation. And, so that we can be people who solve life's problems by praise and who lead others in discovering the same secret, He gives us the gift of praise. Every relationship, family, friendship, and church—as well as every challenge and opportunity—needs a person whose first inclination is to praise the Lord for what He is doing and wants to do.

Your response to that description may have been, "Lord, I need all the gifts!" Who doesn't? But an evidence of one or several of them may be the Lord's guidance that He will lead us into greater opportunities to grow in the communication of the gifts. The greatest gift of all is love. We can't respond to any guidance without that. And since the Lord doesn't *give* love but *is* Love, the more we are in places and relationships that require His giving, forgiving, unchanging love, the better.

The further step in knowing God's personal will is not singular, but plural. This gift is not just a friend but a carefully guided selection of a small band of prayer partners. We all need a handful of people who are our cheering section as well as coaches in our efforts to do the will of God. These must be friends in Christ who are adventurers in guidance themselves. They must also be people who have no axe to grind for our success or failure. If they have nothing to gain or lose from our choices, they will be people who have no motive in mind but to help us sort out what we are discovering in the Bible, prayer, thought, and feelings about next steps in God's strategy or His guidance in perplexities and problems. They need to be people who have displayed in words and actions that they are for God's best in our life, are for us as people, and are open channels for the Spirit. Added to that, they need to be people who are open to both the encouragement and correction of friends in their own lives. Beware of the "loner" who is in deep fellowship with no one but himself or herself, and is an overloaded storehouse of advice for other people. Such persons have plenty of input for others, but never allow you to penetrate their guarded exterior.

I talked with one of my trusted confidants about a crucial decision I had to make. He's no "yes-man" or an affirmer of something just because I want to do it. He listened carefully, probed with questions, and helped me check my motives. He shared similar decisions in his own life and related what he had learned. Then we prayed together. My friend was free enough to confide what he thought and felt I should do, but was also free enough as a person not to make that a source of pressure to please him and not God. He called me a week later to give further insight. I felt the Lord's love in his concern. What he shared in both visits had to stand the test of my own prayer alone with God.

There are times when fellowship and prayer groups become our tightly knit group of sharing partners. This is excellent because of the consistency of time together and the centrality of prayer and Bible study as the basis of the group's oneness. Often a next-step decision can be shared with the group for corporate prayer during the meeting, and then individually afterward.

We were not meant to make it alone, without the Lord and His people. His will is that we be brothers and sisters in Him, and encourage and enable each other in the discovery of His will and specific guidance.

The last step I want to suggest in order to find a sure knowledge of God's personal will for us is commitment. It is rewarded with a new friend to many of us—peace. The wedding of commitment and peace has several offsprings: a sense of relief, a sense of hope, and a sense of humor! After all the data are gathered from the Bible, prayer, our thoughts and feelings, and the insights of others, knowing God's personal will necessitates completely letting go of the decision with the clear assurance that God has a plan and is perfectly capable of communicating it to us. When we commit the decision, choice, or uncertainty to Him, the sure sign that we have really relinquished it and know that He has the authority and responsibility to guide our steps is that we feel a profound peace. Our wills are His, and we are free of the terrible tension of thinking we are in charge of everything.

The relief gives us hope that in time and on time we will know what we are to do. Even in the most serious times of our quest for God's personal will, we will find that we have a fresh sense of humor. We can laugh at ourselves and our uptight worry. We are alive forever, and even if we miss one phase of His guidance, we are still in His ultimate will. An old Irishman speaking to a friend on Sunday reflected on the sermon he had heard about faith, hope, and love. "Now abide these three," he said: "faith, hope, and love. And the greatest of these is a sense of humor!" We would disagree with his memory of the text but agree that faith, hope, and love ought to result in seeing the humor in life and in ourselves.

If we slip on a wrong choice instead of striding ahead in the right one, God will be there to catch us. When we get free from the tenseness about getting guidance, finally we are in a condition to receive it.

Here are 12 questions to ask and answer in a practical inventory for making a maximum decision under the Lord's guidance:

1. Is it consistent with the Ten Commandments?

2. Will it deepen my relationship with Christ?
3. Is it an extension of Christ's life, message, and kingdom?
4. If I do it, will it glorify Him and enable me to grow as His disciple?
5. Is there a scriptural basis for it?
6. Is it adventuresome enough to need the Lord's presence and power to accomplish it?
7. Has prolonged prayer and thought produced an inner feeling of "rightness" about it?
8. Is it something for which I can praise Him in advance of doing or receiving it?
9. Is it an expression of authentic love, and will it bring ultimate good in the lives of the people involved?
10. Will it be consistent with my basic purpose to love the Lord and be a communicator of His love to others?
11. Will it enable me to grow in the talents and gifts the Lord has given me?
12. Will my expenditures still allow tithing plus generous giving of my money for the Lord's work and the needs of others?

These are questions I ask. There are many things I have not done because I could not say yes to all 12 of these. Of course, when I look back, the poorest choices and decisions have been made when I didn't ask and answer all of them. But the Lord gives forgiveness and the challenge, "Tomorrow's another day, another chance, and a new beginning!" And so I press on, a great deal more determined to be sure of the 12-way test He's given me.

We have been called by the pleasure of God's will.

Life's ultimate pleasure and sublime joy is to be liberated by God to desire to live in intimate fellowship with Him. That's His will for our lives. Guidance, specific help with daily decisions, and clear direction for each step of the way are thrown in for extra measure—just because He loves us so much!